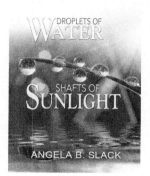

A COLLECTION OF POEMS AND REFLECTIONS

DROPLETS OF
WATER

SHAFTS OF
SUNLIGHT

ANGELA B. SLACK

Droplets of Water
Shafts of Sunlight

by
Angela B. Slack

Select *Arrow*
PUBLISHING

Droplets of Water Shafts of Sunlight

 Published in the UK by SelectArrow Ltd.
www.selectarrow.net

ISBN: 978-1-7398830-1-0

Cover and interior design: Homer Slack
Editor: Angela Slack

Dedication

This book is dedicated to my village who has nurtured my shattered spirit back to wholeness, loved me unconditionally, disciplined me, prayed me through trials, cheered me on, and set a standard of righteousness and integrity in my life. I love you all.

Posthumously I salute: - my mother, **Casita Isolyn Golding-Thompson.** Without whose sacrifice, none of this would have been possible, I love you, mummy. However, It was **Claris Hendriks-Golding** my grandmother whose life of prayer and worship most profoundly and indelibly imprinted Jesus' personage upon my heart. I learned to love Jesus and worship through music as my love language from her. Her advent spirit made me constantly cognisant of the imminence of Jesus' return and I, therefore, needed to live accordingly. Thank you Granny, for teaching me to fear Jehovah God above all others, never to be impressed by anything or anyone that falls beneath His standard of excellence. I know you are in glory playing your harmonica, rocking in an exquisitely beautiful rocking chair with the Angels cheering you on. Play on Granny, play on ...Oh God bless your soul; I am eternally grateful!

To the other deceased: **Patricia Daley, Marjorie Dixon,** aunt **Esmie,** uncle **Glasford** and **Ann-Marie Golding, Cynthia Nugent, Beverly Valentine-Walcott** and **Harold Egbert Walton.** I'm comforted in knowing that your souls are in the magnificent presence of our God. Faithful servants, enjoy your sweet response. I am determined to finish strong and see you all in glory.

Acknowledgements

Thanks to my family and friends who consistently supported me throughout the seasons of my life. Firstly, my brother, **Clive Thompson, OD**; who fathered me, and my sister **Norma Thompson-Mitchell**. My niece **Bianca Mitchell-Glasgow**. Your love and acceptance of me into the Thompson family with all my foibles made life easier. Your advocacy for me taught me the value of doing what is right, no matter what the personal cost. Thanks, my family. God's justice will always prevail!

My dear husband **Homer Slack**, God's greatest gift to me, you have been the steadiest life's companion anyone could ask for and the most tangible picture of what Jesus looks like in my life. Thanks for the many lessons and the shared experiences, I wouldn't trade them.

Dorian and **Briana Slack** my double portion of joy and hope; God knew I would have quit so many times if not for you two. Your youthful perspective and candor helped me to grow in ways I couldn't imagine. I planted and Jesus brought forth a good harvest in you. I am so proud of the adults you have become. Love Jesus and serve Him above all others. Love, mummy.

'Sistah-friends' for life - **Sharon Bett**, my sister-in-law **Shirley Slack-Brown, Sanchia Burrell, Cathy-Ann Clemetson, Debbie Clue, Michelle Goldourne, Delcy Harmit, Sharon Neath, Lorri-Ann Nicholas, Opal Nugent, Joanna O'gilvie, Claudette Simpson, Nicole` Walton- Thompson, Heather Whyte** and [the late] **Jennifer Wood**. My covenant brothers, **David Clemetson, Douglas Cupidon, Milton Mcculloch, Dino Nicholas, Mark Wedderburn,** and **Steve Whyte**; together we built our families.

My mentors, **Errol and Gloria Bean,** Godparents, **Lt. Cmdr. John McFarlane** and **Deanna Mcfarlane,** mother-in-law, **Marcia Cunningham,** and Pastor **Maureen Hanson,** I want to be like you when I grow up. Please don't stop praying for me.

Endorsement

Seventy-five years is relatively a long time; that is the number of years, collectively, that we, the Beans (Errol Bean and Gloria Bean) have been acquainted with the author, Angela B. Slack.

We have empathetically trudged with her through the many revolving seasons of her colourful life's journey; interacted with her as she navigated the highs and lows, the mountains and the valleys, the plains and the plateaus of her physical, emotional and, importantly, her spiritual livity; we have laughed and cried with her; we have prayed for her and her family when she was confronted with destiny, helped determine forks on her path; and yes, we have celebrated her victories with her.

As a teacher of history at the Queen's School (from 1980 – 2012), I recall that Angela Thompson, who entered the Queen's School at the first form in 1982, graduated with the class of '87 and later at sixth form, 1989. I had the honour of teaching her history from the fourth form to the sixth form. Angela was a "bright spark" among an outstanding batch of sixth-form students that promised and actually produced future leaders in many spheres of service. I have watched her transformative approach to being a head girl of the school, serving as the Valedictorian and Salidictorian respectively.

As a student of history, Angela exhibited natural brilliance; she was dramatically expressive and innovative, precocious and loquacious; yet, notwithstanding her dynamic, engaging, and at times, animated personality, she enjoyed an excellent rapport with her fellow students and her teachers equally.

I have proudly followed her academic career to being an honours graduate of the University of the West Indies (Mona), BA Hons (History and International Relations), and subsequently, successfully completed the post-graduate Dip

Ed. (Drama In History teaching). As the HOD of the History-Social Studies Department, I was most delighted to welcome Angela when she returned to the Queen's School as a teacher. I am not too surprised that she has morphed into a writer/publisher and now a poet of note. I, Gloria N. Bean, "Her Teacher," am honoured and grateful to be included as one of her teachers to whom she pays tribute with a heart-warming poem, *"The Sum of You = Me!"*

"My heart was aching for answers to questions of my ancestors,
Along came my mentor, Gloria Been espousing History;
She excavated me and revealed hidden within was a repository,
Sufficient to hold the treasures of the truth of Caribbean History, for posterity.
She showed me that my mind was a doorway to galaxies, of discoveries..."

As a fellow writer/poet, I, Errol D. Bean, have had the privilege to read the draft manuscript of *"Droplets of Water – Shafts of Sunlight."* In this Angela's first anthology of 50 meticulously selected poems, one each to mark her season of fifty cycles around the sun; the author uses the motif of the four climatic seasons to illustrate her own journey while simultaneously engaging her readers to script the narrative of their own journey in their minds.

She writes:
"I believe (the collection) best represents the different seasons of my life (and perhaps yours too) which run parallel to the natural seasons of Spring, Summer, Autumn and Winter. It was the calm, insistent voice of the Holy Spirit of God that spoke to me through nature and circumstances."

In her insightful introduction, Angela, opens her heart, mind and soul in an 'honest to God' summary of her journey.

"My physical and emotional healing is a work in progress; I am not where I was yesterday nor am I the same person; thanks be to God."

Her language is picturesque and colourful; lovers of language usage should find this collection satisfying:
"...glorious moments in the sunshine: the smell of balsam in the trees, the sound of the wind rustling through the leaves, the smell of freshly fallen rain, the glorious sight of barley swaying in the breeze and birds flitting and chirping happily from tree to tree, the green cathedral that is in the canopy of tall trees and the entire world that was beneath my feet as I trod on the insect kingdom..."

The healing power of nature, poetically captured by the creative outflow from Angela,
"I had found my therapy, meters from my doorstep, it was exhilarating and FREE!"

In her Preface: "What is in a Day?" Angela, cites an interesting comparison between each moment of a day and the pixels of a photo:
"Each day is made up of tiny moments. Like individual threads are woven into a tapestry and pixels make up a picture, similarly, each moment makes up our day."

Mindfulness is hinted at,
"I am therefore resolved to be very present in every moment of my life and cherish each memory."

But in addition to satisfying the appetite of lovers of language usage, or perhaps, beyond that object, Angela's higher purpose is to challenge readers to settle their personal account with the Creator of the seasons; she admonishes us,
"These Winter poems invite us (individually and collectively) to take stock of the frailty and finiteness of life; may they inspire

you to settle your accounts with our Creator; I have!"

If I were to select one poem to recommend as a "not to be missed read," difficult as it is, it would be *"Note to Self"* (No. 12); an absolutely magnificent poem that takes humour to a new and different level; it's a poem of harmony with self in a wholesome way.

It is against the background of our collective foundation connection with the author, Angela; it is as a fellow writer/poet and because of my personal love for her writing style, and as her former teacher/mentor, respectively, that we take pleasure in unreservedly endorsing this anthology: *"Droplets of Water – Shafts of Sunlight."*.

In our opinion, this publication is not just another 'run-of-the-mill' anthology, but one that we believe, will be a useful addition to the extensive body of poetic works worldwide; we also believe that this anthology will inspire honest reflection on the significance of the stages of one's physical development and chronological age-stage; but also importantly, we believe that it will challenge us all to take an honest check on the lessons to be learned, spiritually, from each season we experience as we navigate the cycles and stages of life.

It is our prayer that the Spirit of the Most High Almighty God will empower and use *"Droplets of Water – Shafts of Sunlight"* as a conduit of hope and spiritual renewal to everyone who interacts with each poem.

Errol D. Bean – The Thinking Bean,
Author/Minister/Poet/Songwriter.

Gloria N. Bean – Her Teacher,
Retired teacher/Lecturer,
St Catherine, Jamaica.

Endorsement

The art of gently pouring out one's soul onto the pages of a book has been lost in an age of instantaneous communication where the unchecked power to ventilate one's feelings to the world, without thought or reservation, is a few clicks away.

'Droplets of Water and Shafts of Sunlight' is an uplifting reminder that we cannot divest ourselves of the patience required to birth an important literary work that heals brokenness and affirms human frailty. Like *A Very Stout Tree,* Angela, the main witness to her life story, has braved the elements that define each season of her kaleidoscopic life. She has indeed paid homage to God in *Ode to the Creator* and has left me feeling that *It's Okay Not to Be Okay* while *Screaming Into the Wind* as long as I learn to *Laugh Again.*

This work is emblematic of an emotionally evolved imperfect human being who, *Pushing Through the Pain,* has unequivocally told us that we are all capable of moving through life's seasons and their untamed peculiarities and yet retaining our *Identity.* This soul Sistah has embraced her own vulnerability and has, with uncommon courage, told us that the experiences of our lives do not define us, but that we, the authorised autobiographers, defy them in our storytelling.

This poetic reflection is a must-read as it is long-awaited therapy for those who thought their story was too ugly to be told. Within its pages is a message for the emotionally avoidant, the conflict-averse, the resolutely hopeless, the accidental reader, and of course, the endangered aesthete. Simply put, this is 'beauty for ashes' in a book that delivers free *Life Lessons* paid for in full by its author.

Her Hon. Miss Sanchia - Gay Burrell,
St. Andrew, Jamaica.

Endorsement

A poetic memoir, that is what *'Droplets of Water, Shafts of Sunlightlight'* is. Angela B. Slack bares her life and her soul. It is not always pretty but it is deeply moving. Tragedy and hopefulness spun together like a tangled web. Tragedy stands tall but hope runs deep. There is hope nurtured by faith, nurtured in faith with religious conviction encountering dissonance. Actions, feelings, ideas, beliefs, and values are part of a corrugated whole. Ridges and grooves that appear not to fit cognitively do, emotionally and psychically.

Yet there is beauty, much to savour as the human spirit defies limitations and constraints to soar. Grace transforming pain, grief salved by human tenderness and divine unction. The highs and the lows are a lot, but never too much, not overpowering for Intensity is tempered by a tranquil spirit.

Jamaica and England, birthplace, and current residence form the backdrop. Home, family, spirituality, and profession form the context. Each touches the other, informs, and sometimes competes with another. Nostalgia there is, almost a longing but not quite looking back as there is hope for the future. The longing is for redemption, wholeness, and completion.

Angela Slack writes for those who struggle with self, meaning, and purpose. Who doesn't? Perhaps the mindfully lazy. Those who flit through life short of reflection, void of a praying spirit, emptied of self-awareness. The best of us know the dark night of the soul. The closer we are to the divine, the more we realize how much we lack. "Woe is me, for I am undone." Light redeems but it exposes. "A city set upon a hill cannot be hid." The rest (most of us) see a spark, get a glimpse. We know there is more to life even if we reject, refuse, revolt, turn our backs or run away. We know! Yes, we know!

We are privileged to be invited on this personal journey. We may not be worthy, all of us but each gets an invite. So, we accept it with grace and with gratitude. We may smile, laugh, cry, weep, holler, whatever. It is a worthwhile journey.

What a journey!

Eron Henry,
Communications Consultant,
Communications and Media Manager,
Lott Carey, USA.

Endorsement

Angela B. Slack is passionate, 'out of the box', and insanely in love with Jesus. In *Droplets of Water and Shafts of Sunlight*, she powerfully chronicles her journey with the Lord. She candidly reveals the heart of God through her own life stories, not holding back any punches. Angela in her inimitable style, not only shows her successes but her failures, pain, and triumphs. This is not just a book of poems; it is a road map to successfully traverse the seasons of life.

Read this and become empowered to experience and overcome life's greatest challenges, whilst experiencing the grace of God Himself.

Dino B. Nicholas,
Senior Pastor,
Maranatha Ministry International,
Kingston, Jamaica.

Endorsement

Seasons come and seasons go and Angela B. Slack has given us a glimpse of how these can affect one's life either negatively or positively. However, as I absorbed myself in these tear-filled, yet happy, inspiring, motivating, and captivating poems, It was clear to me that seasons don't define our author's disposition owing to the fact that her life is defined by being complete in God alone.

Good Morning Daddy! This is inspirational and a reflection for me when I wake every morning; and this held my enthusiasm throughout the pages of this book. This poem shows how connected to the VINE the author is, so much so that she acknowledges this great DADDY who is always present. *It Was Always God,* from the moment of Angela's inception tells me that all she is and was is encompassed in a creative, mighty, and awesome God. If you read, *Mamma and the Child,* and you never knew your mother, but was adopted and at your stage in life you still feel the rejection and the abandonment; just remember that weeping may endure for a night but joy comes in the morning. The author invites us to *Push Through the Pain,* feed the spirit man, and embrace the healing touch of Jehovah Rapha to a place called Victory.

All the poems written by our author represent someone's testimony, someone's experiences of abuse, someone's healing from a disgraceful trauma, someone's deliverance, and someone's acceptance of our Creator God. I encourage everyone to grab hold of this book because each page prompts the reader to see their own frailty and dependence upon an external God who is always present in our circumstances and situations. I wholeheartedly endorse this book '*Droplets of Water and Shafts of Sunlight*' written by Angela B. Slack.

Dr. Cynthia Patricia Noble,
Founder Praise Academy of Dance, Jamaica, and Barbados.
Former Artistic Director, Praise Academy of Dance Jamaica,
Dance Instructor, Praise Academy of Dance,
Mandeville, Jamaica.

Foreword

People Change, so says Angela B. Slack in her poem (No. 25) of the same name.

If anyone can claim that as true, Angela B. Slack can. The poetry and prose emerging from her inner being and presented here are a completely true and honest reflection of her life. Holding nothing back for fear of pain, embarrassment or criticism, Angela has penned in simple but beautiful words, experiences from her own life that are the unspoken and often repressed reality of so many. Through this volume of poetry, she gives a voice to the voiceless, hope to the hopeless, joy to the joyless, and brings a deep-seated warmth and smile to the hearts and faces of all who read her work.

Using the four seasons of the year as the pallet for her works, she paints a literary montage ranging from the refreshing rejuvenation of Spring following the harsh cold of Winter, through the joys of youthful summers in Jamaica, the grandeur of Autumn colours, the emotional healing of exploring nature's forests, to the sure life-transition to winter. Her poetic approach of entwining within those seasons the mixture of treasured friendships, painful relationships, and the ultimate acceptance of self-operating in unswerving trust in God's divine providence permeating the lives of herself, her husband, her children, and their ministry is notable in this collection.

I am privileged and honoured at being asked to write this Foreword, and do so with great happiness. I know you will enjoy this collection of poems.

Lt. Cdr. John McFarlane, OD, JP.
St. Andrew, Jamaica.

Table of Contents

Spring

Summer

Autumn

Winter

Preface

What is in a Day?

"Seize the day, put little trust in tomorrow." Horace

Have you ever seen the beauty in a single droplet of water as it hangs precariously on a random leaf or as it runs down a windowpane or have you ever seen the spectrum of colour as a shaft of sunlight intersects a droplet of water? The spectrum of colour is so beautiful and these tiny moments are all a part of God's masterpiece painting, His living tapestry. We need to step back to see the whole as well as we need to look close to witness these moments as nature unfolds the glory of God.

I have recovered from a recent back injury that had me bedridden and praying for pain-free days and the time when I could walk again to return. I longed to see what the outside looked like. The same landscape that was just outside my window was inaccessible to me. I'd come to take it for granted until I couldn't see it anymore. I cried out to God, "Father will this be my portion? Will I just lie here for the rest of my days, on my back?" God's answer was, "You will walk again but I had to put you on your back to get your attention." Well, to say the least, He certainly had my attention then.

Miracles in Every Moment

Once I was able to ambulate again, I took on walking with a dear, late friend, Barry Freer. I had to "push through the pain", the doctor told me. So I did, oh my days, what miraculous tiny moments I saw as I walked slowly, literally learned to take tiny steps again, until I could walk 5-6 kilometres with ease.

Barry encouraged me to keep walking in the nearby woods in particular and 'just be' with the trees. He went on so much about it, I had to look it up and I found out, it is really a thing called *Shinrin-yoku.*

> *"Tree bathing/forest bathing is proven to lower heart rate and blood pressure, reduce stress hormone production, boost the immune system, and improve overall feelings of wellbeing... Forest air doesn't just feel fresher and better— inhaling phytoncide seems to actually improve immune system function."*[1]

Once I began, I realised I had missed these glorious moments in the sunshine: the smell of balsam in the trees, the sound of the wind rustling through the leaves, the smell of freshly fallen rain, the glorious sight of barley swaying in the breeze and birds flitting and chirping happily from tree to tree, the green cathedral that is in the canopy of tall trees and the entire world that was beneath my feet as I trod on the insect kingdom. The therapy I received from nature was priceless, worth more than the many painkillers a day, the physiotherapy, and the acupuncture I had to be subjected to each week. Well, I couldn't be more chuffed. I had found my therapy, meters from my doorstep, it was exhilarating and FREE!

Make Every Day Count!
Turning 50 has made me very reflective and introspective, and the one thing I have learned is that the past is physically lost and only virtually retrievable from the fog of memory. However, what I do have is the wonderful gift of a new day. Each day is made up of tiny moments. Like individual threads are woven into a tapestry and pixels make up a picture, similarly, each moment makes up our day. We are often missing majestic, meaningful, tiny moments each day as we rush through life. We need to literally stop and smell the roses, and pause for a cause.

1. https://en.wikipedia.org/wiki/Nature_therapy

I became painfully aware of this when I was so busy with my professional life that I missed key moments in my children's development and try as hard as I could; I couldn't get them back. I was broken-hearted. I was doing my part to look after them by earning an income but they needed me more than things. So, my first lesson was to invest in people, not things and I had to begin with my own two little people.

Thank God for supportive friends who pointed it out and who were there to fill some of those gaps so that my children didn't feel bereft. Once I realised what was happening I gave up the career path that I was on; it just wasn't worth it. I moved houses, changed my job, and attempted to salvage the situation by intentionally making the remaining days that I had with my children count. Phew, I felt like I had dodged a bullet. God's grace gave me a second chance and I took it.

Therefore, I see each day as an opportunity to learn something new about life and about myself. My mother used to say to me, the words of an old proverb;

"There are three things that never return –
- The speeded arrow
- The spoken word
- A day that is spent."

As a child, I was not quite sure what the meaning or the relevance of this wise saying was but now in the autumn of my life, its meaning is crystal clear. Yesterday is gone, tomorrow is not guaranteed, now is all that matters. I am therefore resolved to be very present in every moment of my life and cherish each memory.

So my dear readers as you read my reflections on life, and this collection of poems, my prayer for you is that you too will be resolved to be reflective and proactive in your daily living.

I encourage you to cherish each precious moment, capture the awesomeness in every season, ponder the lessons in every experience, learn them well and count the blessings of every new day.

Yes, live life fully, laugh heartily, love completely and forgive absolutely.

Love as always,

Angela

Introduction

I have put this special collection of poems and reflections on life together to share with you aspects of my personal journey according to the seasons of life. This was the most effective way that I found that I could describe my life's journey and chronicle some of my personal experiences to date. There were times when the information was just too emotionally overwhelming and consequently, my summary and analysis of what I had learned during my journey have been encapsulated in the body of these poems and accompanying reflections. My physical and emotional healing is a work in progress. I am not where I was yesterday nor am I the same person; thanks be to God.

This book Droplets of Water Shafts of Sunlight, I believe best represents the different seasons of my life (and perhaps yours too) which run parallel to the natural seasons of Spring, Summer, Autumn, and Winter. It was the calm, insistent voice of the Holy Spirit of God that spoke to me through nature and circumstances. God knew that being the avid nature lover that I am, this analogy would make practical sense to me and resonate with readers, especially nature lovers.

Upon reflection, I have lived through the boundless energy, forthrightness, and naivete of Spring. I learned a lot of information about many subjects; my head was crammed with facts but I had gained very little wisdom from all my learning. Hopefully, you will see your childhood self here too as you read the poems of Spring.

The section on Summer contains poems that depict passionate love and adult experiences; many painful lessons learned, and heartbreaks that helped me to grow up fast, adding experience to knowledge that taught me wisdom. The poems in this section hopefully, will inspire you to rise above those kinds of setbacks with humour and resilience.

I believe that I am now in the Autumn of my life, being a "Queenager", enjoying this decade of settled wisdom and lessons well learned. Autumn is like a new Spring, we are old enough to do as we please and are fully aware of the consequences of all our choices; we tend to choose with wisdom. We become unhurried having at this stage nothing to prove; rather, we enjoy the freedom to be ourselves. Isn't it exhilarating?

It is my prayer that these poems will help you, in a personal way, to find yourself and establish a clear identity with the help of God who knows you best, having created you with purpose and for His glory.

Then, at last, eventually, the long Winter sleep will come and we should all anticipate it with wisdom and prepare. Perhaps like you, I am not quite there yet. However, the old adage says, "Time waits on no one," So, "I must not [just] count the days but make the days count!"[1]

These Winter poems invite us individually and collectively to take stock of the frailty and finiteness of life; they inspire you to settle your account with our Creator; I have!

---

1 Muhammad Ali. https//muhammadalicenter.org

SPRING...

A lovely reminder of how
beautiful change can truly be.

Unknown

What Spring Means To Me...

Springtime is a season of firsts and the chance for new beginnings. Growing up on the tropical Island of Jamaica I never fully appreciated the wonderful gift of Spring; until I came to live in a temperate climate in the United Kingdom. Once you have lived through four to five months of grey skies, cold, wet, and dreary days you will surely long for the return of clear blue skies that offset the beautiful colour pallet of Spring. Who wouldn't rather look out the window and hear bird songs and see butterflies flitting from fruit to tree, see green grass, trees fully clothed with various flowers and laden with leaves?

Spring takes me back to my problematic beginnings, my years of early childhood trauma, and my battle with the concept of family. It reminds me that no matter what harm I have experienced, what cruelty was done to me, or what dysfunction was in my foundation, it doesn't define me because in God there is always another season and opportunity to look forward to. Spring means to me, the promise of another opportunity to keep growing and learning and blossoming into who God has made me to be.

Springtime means change is inevitable and good; not something to be afraid of but rather worthy to be embraced. It comes every year, interestingly, right after Winter. Thank God for Spring!

Poem 1

ODE TO THE CREATOR

Written on a Spring morning while lying in bed, just meditating on God's goodness. In my spirit, I began travelling around the globe seeing all the moments recorded in the poem below. I called my husband Homer to record it as I described what I was seeing unfolding. When he read it back to me, we both just marvelled at the majesty of God's Creation. This book later borrowed its title from its first line and this collection of poetry began – the 24th of June 2012.

Droplets of water, shafts of sunlight,
Peals of thunder,
Starlit night,
Oceans spray, angel's ray,
Calm green meadow, first light of day.
Midnight dew, dusky dawn,
Twilight hue, life reborn!

Skylark cries, green grass whispers,
Eagles fly, kitten whiskers,
Fluffy tail, strong bulking frame,
Long elegant mane.
Butterfly kisses, shooting star wishes,
Rainbow swashes, moonbeam watches,
Changing seasons, eternal reasons.
Worldwide symphony, cosmic epiphany,
Terrestrial songs and ethereal throng;
Join in testifying,
Yahweh is one!

Mountain top table, ice-capped peaks,
Plunging valleys, livestock roaming rambling fields.
Bounty filled meadows, small critters at play,
Ice lakes and glaciers, whale spout spray.
Penguins applaud, ice crabs scamper,
Old sea lions awake from their repose;
Bear cubs sneezing honey from their nose.

From clump of earth, throughout all the Milky Way,
To distant galactic stars,
All living things worship and say,
Yahweh, how awesome You are!

Poem 2

GOOD MORNING DADDY

I've opened my eyes, I've breathed in and out consciously,
The first thought that runs into my conscious mind is YOU;
My Heavenly Daddy.
I roll out of bed and sitting up, I greet You first of all,
This simple prayer is my first port of call.
"Good Morning Daddy"- is the first thing I say,
Followed by, "What do You have in store for me today?"

The sound of Your voice at the day's dawning,
A tug on my heart of destiny's calling,
To fulfill Your purposes here on earth,
Give this mortal life it's worth.
Awakened by the morning sun's rays on my face.
I swing my windows open wide,
My lungs fill with fresh air and joy fills me inside.
It's Your air I'm breathing Daddy,
I'm as thankful as can be.

Aww, It was rainy throughout the night watches,
The earth is sodden through,
See the swaying plants giving thanks to You?
Birds chirping, fluttering from fence to the big Buddleia tree,
Here comes the sociable Madame butterfly,
Followed by Mr stripey pants himself - Mr. Bumblebee,

Not every day is easy to face,
Especially when there is so much to do,
I feel overwhelmed and daunted about getting through.
Each task is like a mountain, housework is so ungrateful, it's
never done;
But one thing I'm glad for is that I can greet each day with the
Son;
Of God, who died for me who is always in my heart never more
than a whisper away,
Always listening to my thoughts and answering my prayer every
day.

Good Morning Daddy!
This simple greeting means so much to You and me,
It's the acknowledgment of our deep connection,
The mystical paternity of You for me.
Good morning Daddy!
It never gets old,
It never gets burdensome, each new day that I greet You,
New wonders around me unfold.
It gives me such confidence that You are with me,
My day is powered by your delegated authority.
Others have their 'Energizer' batteries, generators of electricity,
But Daddy, I have You and You are all I need.

Poem 3

IT WAS ALWAYS YOU

This poem was inspired by Psalm 136. It reminds us of how God never left His people and as I meditated on His goodness, the incidents of my eventful journey through life came rolling back into my consciousness and I heard my heart rise in grateful worship and say... It was always You. Written the 8th of February 2021.

It was always You,
From the moment of inception,
In Your mind.

It was always You,
From the instance of conception,
In Your heart.

It was always You,
From the time of gestation,
Nine months in Your care,
In the womb of You.

Yes, You -my Creator,
Yes, You -my Father,
Yes You -my Redeemer,
You were always there.

In the circumstance of my birth,
Throughout my struggles with self-worth,
Your validation and qualification,
Of me, who I am, whose I am,
My Celestial paternity,
You were always there.

Loss of direction,
Creative stagnation,
Poor health and deterioration,
Of mind, body, and soul,
You were STILL there.

Being misunderstood, manipulated,
Abused and alienated,
Disappointed, Oh, the pain in my soul,
You were reassuringly there.

The long road to freedom,
The lonely walk of integrity,
The letting go of expectations placed on me,
The resident You within me,
You were consistently there.

At the end of my tether,
Every task a burden, a bother,
Overwhelmed, out of steam,
Tempted to let go of my dream,
You were right there,
Edifying me.

'All churched out',
So tired of 'friendly fire',
Warfare debilitated me,
I just wanted to be set free,
Of religious hypocrisy.

You rescued me, you reached down,
Scooped me up and held me,
Loved me so intensely and intimately,
You NEVER left me!

Yes, the wisdom was Yours,
The power to make the right choices,
Steadying me from slipping or quitting,
Your favour promoted me above my peers,
You gave me insight beyond my years,
Always amazingly, shining through me.

You alone were with me in the hour of oppression,
You were the light that dispelled the darkness,
In the deep dungeon of depression.
You emboldened me,
You rejuvenated me.
You reinforced my capacity to stand and resist the enemy,
You gave me a resounding VICTORY!
My Father God, You alone,
You were always there with me.

Poem 9

BEING GOD

I wonder; is it hard being God?
It must be hard being God,
I can hardly cope with just being me,
Chores, duties, responsibilities,
Keeping up, staying afloat, landing the proverbial boat,
Balancing the books,
Bringing home the bacon,
Maintaining my looks.
The struggle is really REAL,
Breathing in and out is hard,
And living for God is the ultimate BIG deal.
God, how do You do it?

Humanity, perspicacity, tenacity,
Incessant demands, complaints,
And rebellious opinionatedness.
A cosmos filled with planets,
Earth: flora, fauna, and animals,
All living things in air and sea,
Such vastness and enormity,
Yet knowing every droplet of water,
Every shaft of sunlight,
Every leaf that floats on the wind,
And every fruit that falls from a tree,
Oh, woe! Woe, is me!
I just couldn't cope with being God,
I'd quit if it were me.

If I were God for a day, I'd be screaming,
"One at a time, wait your turn, no you can't have it;
I said to wait patiently in line!"
Now, that's just too much,
Too much to think about, to plan, to adjust.
Too much to balance, allow/disallow, give free run/curtail,
Delete, delete, just delete!
There'd be no humanity left, if it was up to me.

God, Great God, Omnipotent, Omniscient, Immortal, Invisible,
Sensitive, Caring, Tender, Loving God.
Creator, Master, Planner, I bow in adoration,
Shout in adulation, Awesome God!
How do You, do You?
I wouldn't dare try, I wouldn't want to,
I just couldn't manage the massive responsibility.
I'm baffled by my fellows who 'spit at the sky' and curse You,
Who'd rather die in ignorance,
In arrogant stupidity,
Questioning Your very divinity,
Please, pity their simplicity.

It is clearly very hard to be God
From the perspective of my finite humanity,
But to actually BE GOD is elementary,
A mere flick of a finger,
A thought, a spoken word,
And all becomes a reality.
Being God, to God, is His nature,
So for Him, it's just plain easy.
Am glad I am not God;
I couldn't be.
Thank You, God,
That You are God,
And not feeble me!

Poem 5

DON'T TOUCH MY SISTER

Take your hands off my sister!
Remove your filthy hands from where you touched her!
Can't you see she's confused?
She doesn't understand that what you have done is a violation
Of her as a human and a woman, child.
Yes, a child, which makes what you have done reprehensible and
vile.

Don't shoot? You had better just scoot. If you don't leave now
you will surely pay,
I swear that if you ever show up again around here I'll…
Momma, don't say another word, I know what I saw, right there
in situ,
Leave, now, just go! Take your evil aura and your psychosis with
you,
Don't let the doorknob hit you, where the... Or I swear I'll…

Meanwhile, eyes filled with confusion quietly sitting to one side,
the assaulted child,
I have to protect her or else who will when her brother is not
there?
I have to hurry and grow up, who else will stand up, to protect
this child right here?
There, there now, a barrier against all the men in the world is
firmly in place.

12

I will never forget the look of shock on my brother's face,
He feared what would have happened if he'd been too late.
My brother is the only decent man in the human race.

I loved him so completely at that moment,
When he stood up for me, pointing my 'uncle's' gun at him,
The heathen, the philistine who was caught within,
Jesus, am I a dirty girl? Why did uncle touch me in that way?
Why was my brother filled with such outrage?
Was I wrong, was he angry at me?
My brother, who defended and protected my dignity.

Left just sitting in my disgrace, averted eyes, no one met my gaze,
The hired help took me away to bathe and change,
No one said a word about it ever again.
After all, that was then, this is today.
The nightmare will end if we all just pretend.

Poem 6

MAMMA AND 'THE CHILD'

I had this lucid dream in 2002, not long after arriving in the UK from Jamaica. That night when I became aware that it was only a dream I was so heartbroken because I had not had an opportunity to have closure with my Mother's untimely demise. I missed her terribly but life just went on as I was almost 8 months pregnant at the time of her passing. I was terrified to vent my feelings of grief and chose anger instead. I somehow had the idea in my head that if I cried I would hurt my unborn child. So I kept it all in. That night was the closing of the door to the past in so many ways. Momma had passed but I had a little daughter and a new life to embark on, in a new country. It was a new mountain to climb but the promise of a very different view beckoned me. Written the 30th of August 2002.

Mamma, Mamma is that you, the only bosom that I knew?
I was sure I smelt your perfume, felt your presence in my room.
Grasping desperately in the darkness, at an iridescent hue,
Tear-soaked pillow, deflated hope, heartbreak, and gloom.
Hearing your voice, conjuring your image, your smile,
But it never lasted, still segregated,
Mamma and 'The Child.'

My Mother? I never knew her, fate kept me from her side,
Why should an innocent suffer the penalty of her parent's crime?
Adoption? So troublesome, what a scandal and trial?
"Insanity Cassie, disregarding your family for this bastard child!"
Yet, Mamma loved me, absolutely, despising prejudice and false pride.
"Your Honour, grant me custody; in my heart this child is mine."

Family? Exploit me, next-door neighbour assault me,
Still loving unconditionally, doing errands for everybody,
"Shut up you ingrate! You're a liar, you're wicked and a fool!"
"No, not me! I am a Christian child and I am doing well in school,"
I'm Head Girl, valedictorian, I've passed my exams with distinctions,"
College, university! Mamma, at least you were so happy.
Yet, my 'family' still disregards me and offers no congratulations.

The years fly past, the worst has come too fast,
Mamma, you've gone and left me alone with these snakes in the grass,
How am I to cope alone? Will I be able to function?
Mamma was my hope, chief cheerleader, my inspiration.

Can't manage the pain, choose anger instead,
Look, the 'ole hypocrites, those same ones titivating the dead.

Mamma, what good is all this fuss over your makeup and
shroud?
If when you needed them in your sickness, they were nowhere
to be found?
Death has no mercy, it claims its victim and takes a bow,
Its timing is awful, Mamma will never see my unborn child now.
Ahhh, but she's only sleeping, still regal like a queen,
Her beautiful face, elegant hands crossed, so very serene.

Passively observing her children attending and processing,
Keeping up appearances, meanwhile, childhood trauma
repressing,
Internal screams of Mamma don't leave me! Only her spirit can
hear it;
I'm already gone my dear, only my body remains, let them have
it.
Even in death, I can't claim her, I shall always the borrower be,
That's okay, I proudly remain indebted to her for all eternity.

Mamma, I'm overwhelmed with grief, using anger to suppress it
Think of the little one inside you, please release every bit of it."
I'll do my best mamma, as usual, you are right,
You sound so happy mamma and you are glowing, so bright.
I'm in heaven now my darling, I'm reflecting God's light.
I miss you so much, mamma.
Love you too darling, sweet dreams and good night.

Poem 7

WEEPING WILLOW TREE

After a wonderful day spent with a dear prayer partner learning with her how to have a prayer walk and talk time with Jesus, I was left quite serene and still. I lingered in that place that exists between the spirit realm and our world wanting to stay there. My friend, realising I was having an experience 'In the Spirit' asked me- "What did you see Angela?" I told her, "A Willow Tree." She replied and responded, "Maybe it's you." It was after she had left me that day that it occurred to me that she was right when she said to me that the Weeping Willow Tree was indeed me. Written the 24th of September 2019.

I saw myself in a daydream, or was it a vision?
There I was standing tall, swaying in the wind,
My willowy, lock-like branches swaying elegantly in the breeze,
I heard the laughter of the wind, the chatter of the birds,
Others' harmonies filled the air, their habitat was me.
Long spindle-like trunk, deep tributary roots well beneath the earth sunk,
Transporting sap and drink to the evergreen leaves that are the glory of me.

I am a Weeping Willow Tree,
I bend and sway with the wind.
I'm flexible and enduring a watcher on the landscape,
I see, hear and feel everything and empathy fills my very being.

Nations have come out of me,
Have been shaded, nurtured,
Dreams entrusted, passions fuelled,
Playing with my branches, wrapped around my trunk,
Resting beneath my shade, humanity has come.

My tears are like vapour carried on the wind,
My groans are my lament,
In my travail I am content,
To bring forth new life each time my intercession is spent,
Watching, guarding, that landscape was me,
A beautiful, weeping, willow tree.

Poem 8

PUSHING THROUGH THE PAIN

Painfully writhing on the floor, my head is spinning,
I'm not gonna lie here just looking at the ceiling,
Pressed face against the windowpane, watching the rain,
I'm gonna get up, suit up, go against the grain,
I'm gonna walk and yes even run again.
Gray day, clouds hang like cobwebs over my foggy brain;
Oh God, no sunshine again?
No worries, I'm gonna push through the pain.

Salty tears splatter shocking me back to reality,
If I just sit here and cry, depression will descend upon me,
Wiping my face with the back of my hand
I'm determined today is the day I will stand,
I'm scared but I'm still determined,
As high as a Jolly Roger on a Pirates' mast,
Lucid moments are few, waking moments blur past,
I'm still gonna push through the pain.

Dramas and food help me medicate my pain,
Tramadol, Gabapentin, Codeine, Morphine,
My new best friends?
NOOO! My reliance on you all must end,
Flesh and blood battle soul and spirit,
An epic clash of forces in my bedroom,

A ringside seat to witness their doom,
FEAR, I've denounced you, leave me now,
Pushing through the pain is my vow.

Jehovah Rapha thanks to You, I'm not afraid,
"You will be pain-free," is what You said!
Choosing a life with truth and worship in it,
Resisting temptation and feeding my spirit.
So my soul and body will follow me,
To a place called VICTORY!
Ahhhhh... the fresh air fills my lungs,
I'm gonna keep pushing until my healing comes.

Poem 9

A BENCH FOR BARRY

❖

Dedicated to the life and legacy of a brother in Christ Barry Freer, who transitioned this life April 27th 2020 during the COVID -19 Pandemic. He will be sadly missed. We were not able to say a proper goodbye due to social distancing regulations but I am confident that he was aware in his spirit how much we loved him and appreciated his friendship. Goodbye dear friend, see you in the eternal woods by the sea of glass, in glory. Written the 5th of May 2020.

21

What does it take to mark the passing of a life?
Better still to keep the memory of them alive?
Is it tears shed when no one is looking,
Is it in groans kept deep inside?
Will loud wailing and beating of the breast do?
Maybe for some people but not for Barry, no, mate not for
you.

The epitaph for Barry is freedom, a life fully lived,
Unrestrained speech, expressed thoughts and laughter,
The epitome of kindness, freshly baked plum bread, a strong
cuppa,
Bear hugs, sloppy kisses, and heartfelt wishes.
He ran life like a marathon always going the distance,
Pacing himself, ensuring he always had more to give,
He lived, loved, and lived, in health and in sickness, he fully
lived!

Hey, Angel come look at this scene, touch that plant, smell
this tree,
Rambling, 'nature' discoveries made by Barry and me,
Two peas in a pod, tagged by others, "as odd as can be,"
We were conjoined in nature, 'tree-hugging' Barry and me.
Scenes of nature unfolding as we chattered and giggled with
glee,
That we'd not missed, the bluebells, daffodils, or robin's song
in Spring.
Barry, Barry wait up, I can't go, oh the pain is too much for
me,
Stop here, rest a minute let's sit awhile and 'just be',
Hey, look at you Angel you've done 5k,
Did you realise how far you walked from where we left the car
today?

Oh wow, Barry, you are my hero,
Thanks for helping me regain my strength and push through
the pain;
You made me get on my feet and walk again and again.
"No biggie, let's go, it will be tea time soon,"
We've been gone all morning and most of the afternoon.

Hey, Barry look it's our favourite 'very stout tree',
I can't keep up Angel, wait a bit, I need to pee,
No worries, Barry, it's only me.
Ready? Let's head back soon or we won't be able to see.

Oh, here we go again another deep 'Barry' question,
I had to stop and really think,
Barry was my teacher as much as he learned from me,
Our classroom was nature, lessons as far as we could see.
Barry, Barry, where are you mate?
You've left me alone to wander among the trees,
To lie alone in the open field and stare at you in glory.

Was that your voice on the wind?
Were you laughing as the breeze rustled through the leaves?
Barry, I'll sit here and remember all that you've ever said to
me.
Here on this bench overlooking the fields of barley,
The blue Lincolnshire sky, the river Freshney running by,
Golden rapeseed fields swaying gently against the azure and
crimson sky,
The rolling sunset across the horizon, joining in concert like
dancers taking their cues,
I'll wait here on this bench, this marker of the friendship of
Barry and me.

Poem 10

A VERY STOUT TREE

*It was a lovely Lincolnshire day in May. The wind was crisp
and the sky endlessly blue. The perfect day to go walking in
the woods and I remember how excited my friend Barry and I
were when we had this encounter with our Very Stout Tree. Like
children, we oohed and ahhed as we hugged it; we laughed that
we dared not even try to climb it but imagined what the view
from it would look like anyway. It immensely dwarfed two grown-
ups like us but regardless we felt so welcomed beneath its
shade. I couldn't wait to get home to write this poem to record
the highlight of our days' adventure. Written the 23rd of MAY
2017.*

We paused to worship, beneath a very stout tree,
Humbled as we gazed up into its green canopy,
Of waving branches and clapping leaves,
Dancing praises to the rhythm of the warm spring breeze.

"What a magnificent shrine," said Barry,
"Ran passed it 50 times and missed its beauty."
So busy clocking our distance my pals and me,
Now, transfixed, by our discovery.

If only it spoke our language or we spoke 'tree',
We could learn of the things it had happened to see,

A silent witness, a recorder of history,
Was our very stout tree.

Over centuries it stood a guardian in sunlight and mist,
Hidden treasures, escapades, battles, lover's trysts,
Rendezvous of covert agents, a place where ramblers remi-
nisced,
Cognizant of things, we being too young, had missed.

Reluctantly we departed,
Quiet reverence in our hearts,
Our silent witness looked upon us,
We realised that worship was its true art.

A testimony of seasons weathered,
A catalogue of catastrophes averted,
A repository of hope unaltered,
A wooden Tabernacle,
A green Cathedral.

Poem 11

IDENTITY

This poem came to me during the third lockdown in the UK. I had so much time to think about the loss of family members and dear friends to COVID -19. Death made me think of my human frailty and ponder my real identity. If I were to die, what would people say had defined me? Written the 29th of January 2021.

My identity is hidden in Christ!
Who I am is not defined by what I do,
Where I was born or the influence I had;
The money I've accumulated,
The learning I've gained or
The people I've associated with,
None of these define me.

I am God's child!
By God's choice to love me,
I was created in His mind,
Everything is inconsequential and secondary,
To my reason for being here
and the plan God has in store for me.

When you see me,
You see grace in place,
Miracles in the making,
Truth at work,

Kindness falling like rain,
Joy keeping me strong,
Worship flowing like a song,
Patience like deep water,
Peace steady like a rock fixed in place,
Justice in progress,
Faith standing still,
A fountain of overflowing grace.

Poem 12

NOTE TO SELF

Mind, Mind wake up its self, it's Me;
Are you kidding? Do you know what time it is in the morning?
I know, I know it's after three.
Come on Mind, cooperate, I need to think things through;
Body needs her beauty sleep, she will be really mad with you.
Trust me, It's important, I am overwhelmed with lists;
You know I am discombobulated when I feel like this.

Well, now that you mention it, you really seem perplexed;
Body doesn't feel so good either, she is tense with stress.
Notepad in hand, Body? Ready, let's go!
You are going too fast, Mind. Please take it slow!
Finally, it's annotated. Gosh, what a list!
Who would have thought there was so much to do?
Yes, it's great when we talk like this.

What's going on, Mind? I am tired and would really like to sleep;
I have tried closing a file which Soul keeps opening up, to peep;
She has been meditating all night.
Really? The irony; sounds like she needs your help with
processing;
Oh, Body, can't you make her sleepy? This is quite taxing!
Add some crying as well, to signal it's time for relaxing.

I am so glad I stayed home tonight and did soul searching;
Seems words can hit as hard as stones and break a heart if
carelessly thrown.
Unforgiveness and hurt gets me so sick;
Mind, you must hurry, help me to resolve it.
"Lord I forgive her,"aah that freed my Soul,
Oh, I have cleared things with Mind, prayed, and cried,
And Body, you seem to have gotten rid of that cold.
Oh, Body, look at you, you have seen better days.
Don't go there, I endured your depression and suffered your
unending raves.

All right, let's get this house in order. Spring cleaning it is;
Let's see: a detox for Body and regular exercise at the gym.
Mind, you need quiet time first thing in the mornings,
Or else how will you fit it all in?
Hey, Soul needs her worship music, a garden filled with sunlight,
A spree of girly shopping and she will be just right.

I think that ought to do it, now let's get back to bed;
I love it when we meet like this, it makes the coming day go full
steam ahead.
Brain, have you got all that? Can you memorise it?
Or, shall Body help you write a list?
Definitely the latter, remember what happened the last time we
were remiss?

This is how we flow together,
The workings of mind, body, and spirit;
The processing, the feeling, and the doing are all a part of it.
None works without the other, it really takes all three;

I've learned to listen in turn, giving expression to all of me.
Especially as I grow older, there is so much more to do;
Time is growing shorter, not just for me but for you too.
The art of self-expression is unique for all;
There are no two persons with the same two spirits, bodies or
minds,
We are all, really one of a kind.

Poem 13

THE SUM OF YOU = ME

I am the sum of the teachers who taught me,
The realisation hit me with incredulity;
Mid-course, I heard my own diction,
Listened to my own instructions,
Marvelled at the echo in my communication.
Who? No less than the late great **Muriel Riley** was speaking
through the sound of me.
She impressed me, she scolded me, "Never willingly bear the
burden of being ordinary,"
She ranted, "Never take your gift for granted, many talented
people are homeless,
Apply yourself, marshall your skills," she never accepted less
than this.
I was never late, always prepared for her class,
I held my breath until I knew I'd passed whatever test, she'd set.
She would never condescend to explain a new word to me,
"Scholars consult their dictionary," today I have her to thank for
my vocabulary,
and so I've taught as she taught me.

At the corner, of her eye was a twinkle almost a wrinkle, a very
shy smile,
When she confidently hitched my wagon to the caravan of
communication,
Of elevated expression that separated me from that which was

31

colloquial,
From street slangs and the gibberish that was spoken glibly in
the streets,
Always educing and soliciting me, to be even better than she?
Couldn't be!

My heart was aching for answers to questions of my ancestors,
Along came my mentor, **Gloria Been** espousing History;
She excavated me and revealed hidden within was a repository,
Sufficient to hold the treasures of the truth of Caribbean History,
for posterity.
She showed me that my mind was a doorway to galaxies, of
discoveries,
Beyond the boundaries of Earth, in the mind of God where my
spirit was birthed;
Where the indomitable spirit of man is beyond bondage and
oppression.
Through the pages of History, I learn that I was born free,
Never to be enslaved again by anybody.
A narrative changer, never accepting women's invisibility,
Choosing rather, to live responsibly and teach many, leaving a
legacy.

Through modern writers, **Helen Bolt** explored the limitations of
existentialism,
She spurred us on to be critical in our thinking.
The epitaphs of lost souls, where things fell apart and did not
hold,
We considered The Pearl of Great Price and whether it was right
To Kill a Mocking Bird.
The power of the spoken word was immortalised in these texts
of modernist writers,

Who were agitators of change, freedom fighters.
Her humour, boldness, and candor advocated for the feminine gender,
Her clarion call of vocation was to scale every wall off of limitation,
To use communication as the means to liberate the soul.

Ethline Aiken a Headmistress and mother who never wore the countenance of bother,
Self-assured, yet cloaked in humility and feminine gentility,
Fair yet firm and fierce in defence of the principles of Christianity.
Upright and kind, never blind to my pubescent instability,
Yet for all my foibles, without prejudice, she allowed me to aspire;
Unselfishly, she championed the best of me.

Violet Thompson Vice-Principal and disciplinarian,
My namesake but not my clan, I was her protégé from day one,
She was so elegant and poised, never a hair out of place, never a voice raised.
The walking epitome of ladylike disposition.
A lover of nature and besotted with aesthetics, she pruned us girls like roses,
Never thinking to teach, I recall how she made good use of me, in History-
"Thompson, carry on!" She'd say, as matters of discipline called her away.
Little did I realise then, I was in teacher training in those formative days.

Audrey DaCosta, if you loved food you loved her,

She oozed the milk of human kindness,
She fondly made such a great cook of me.
I wasn't the best but I loved to eat, so I literally learned by
necessity.
Our own *Martha Stewart* and *Grace Kitchen*'s guru, Lord I loved
her food.
Home Economics was never the same, she'd often proclaim,
Anyone can cook! Cooking never seemed so easy, peasy.
Use all your senses, was no cliché`, the results proved she wasn't
being cheesy.
She floated effortlessly around the Home Economics room,
Smells of good food cooking chasing away adolescent gloom,
Immaculately groomed, so soft-spoken,
You'd never guess cooking was her discipline.

Dreaded P. E. and Netball brings me to my nemesis, **Maureen
Hall**,
Forcing me to run, do long jump and cross-country and worse,
to play field hockey,
Didn't she know, I'm no athlete at all?
I'm what you call a born cheerleader- pom-poms and all,
I was made for dancing tights, tutus, and leotards,
My pleas and petitions were treated with complete disregard.
In retrospect, I laugh at my childhood rancour,
She knew the game of life was already afoot and the scrapes
And bruises, dropped batons and failed passes,
Were toughening us up to face life's catastrophes.
We'd outlast the anonymity and we'd not be phased by fame,
We'd learn the thrill of victory and the agony of defeat,
Yes, those P. E. lessons prepared us to face them as one and the
same.
Now, I thank her for insisting that I try to be all that I could be,

And participate in the game of life to the best of my ability.

Keith Parkin, what an impresario?
At Queens, he was all things dramatic,
He brought out the drama queen in me,
As a Queenager, I cherish the days being at it.
Fond memories of rehearsals and drama classes,
He exposed our talent and cajoled us through our paces.
On the stage, he'd let us lose,
Gave us an outlet for our raging youth.

From Elizabethan to Period Dramas, and Musicals from
Broadway,
I mimed, rehearsed my monologues and soliloquy,
I learned my lines, whatever genre he chose, I was happy to
play.
Mr. Parkin was happy as long as we expressed ourselves and did
it with glee;
He spotted and nurtured the actor and writer in me.
He followed his favourite stage direction and exeunt stage left
I am so bereft, yet I fondly see him treading the eternal boards
in glory.
Adieu and see you soon but not yet, this isn't the last act of my
story.

I was no Picasso but I could draw and paint,
Dennis Souza, my art teacher had such an easy-going
temperament,
I was free to sing while I worked to my heart's content.
The art room was my place of escape, where I was free,
 As long as I completed my assignment, he was happy for me to
be me,

He uncovered talent that to others was unapparent;
But my mother stifled the artist in me,
I was so devastated when she told me,
"You can't take Art at *CXC*."

I learned to put life into perspective,
When colouring in life's scenery,
I drew inspiration from nature's beauty.
I painted the shapes and drew lifelike depictions,
Shaded in the sketches, as life is greater than fiction,
The lifelong lesson is that life is living Art.

Two matriarchs guarded my basic school and primary education,
Gertrude Russell and **Lorna Walker** respectively,
They protected me like a lioness before her cub.
Undoubtedly, without their protection I'd be undone.
They discovered and encouraged my voice,
Learning by rhythm and singing became my choice.
I learned to count and write and was prepared for my common
entrance exams,
Lessons under the trees opened the door of leaning to me,
Sitting on the grass, every learning activity, a pleasant task.
Put to stand on a table at *Y. W. C. A* I sang my heart out loud,
And from that day forward, I was never afraid to face a crowd.

To all my teachers, you were more than I can pen,
You remain in my heart, as much now as back then.
In some way or another, I am here because you bothered,
You endeavoured, to make time, to encourage and nurture my
ability.
I wouldn't be who I am today, without your insistence and
forbearance,

Your sense of personal responsibility that you transferred to me.
My life's work is a vocation, to do my best always,
To have integrity and never be ashamed of who I am and where
I'm from,
To represent my school and my country,
To give the world the best of me.
My beloved teachers, the sum of you = me!

Poem 19

MY SPRINGTIME HAS SPRUNG

My springtime has already sprung,
My striving and struggling to get to the surface of success is
done.
Long gone are my days of being green and wet behind the ears,
They have disappeared over so many years;
And here I am in a new season.

I have the scars, the stretch marks, and shed tears,
The stories to tell, the rhymes and the reasons,
The red flags, the lessons, the landmarks, and blessings.
I have no regrets, I look back in fond nostalgia,
But I wouldn't go back, I can honestly tell ya.

That was then this is now, the past can take its bow.
Plotted all along the road of my life there has been
Enough drama, trauma, and strife.
Thank goodness for the Springtime of youth,
Where indomitability and sheer tenacity are rife.

I had such energy then, I was so strong and fierce;
I learned to fight early to hold my own among family and peers.
All these adversities and challenges made me who I am,
I am today undoubtedly a tried and proven, Warrior Woman.

"Youth is wasted on the Young," they say,
The jury is still out on that, to this day.
For, though the season of my Spring was the youth of me,
It was pretty good then but it was not the best of me,
Tenacity and ambition also need temperance and perspicacity.

Sure, I miss the youthful exuberance,
The enthusiastic optimism, the never-ending drive of sheer will,
But that's a choice we make to grow old and be old,
We can choose to mature and be youthful still.

Though my leaves are turning yellow, auburn, and berry,
And are no longer evergreen,
I have never been merrier to embrace this 'new Spring,'
Because it's boring, being just plain green.
This pallet of Autumn is much more interesting,
Fond farewell Spring.

SUMMER

Some old-fashioned things like fresh air and sunshine are hard to beat.

Laura Ingalls - Wilder

What Summer Means To Me…

Summer, Summer, Summer, means fun in the sun!

Ahh, the joy of knowing that April showers and wet spring days are fully behind me. Leave the 'brolly' and raincoat at home and put on your strappy sandals and get out your sock-imprisoned toes. It's summertime! Feel the warmth of sunshine all over your skin. Long days and late evening sun, mean to me that I have the chance of getting so much more done and I have the added motivation and energy from vitamin D.

The summertime of my life was my years of grafting and building to etch out a future and a career. To make sense of my humanity. I didn't find all the answers or always make the right choices but regardless of the mistakes I have made or how many times I fell down, it's okay, the Son of God was there shining down on me.

Summertime means to me, the audacity to hope and endeavor in the face of daunting circumstances.

Poem 15

SUMMERTIME

*This poem is fondly dedicated to my rambunctious and happy
Golding cousins who contributed to the bulk of my childhood
memories in the summer holidays. Thank you Uncle Glasford
and Aunt Esmie for your warm and welcoming hospitality
and those memorable trips to the St. Elizabeth countryside. I
especially remember Ann-Marie my closest cousin in age and
summertime playmate. Written Summer of 2021.*

Summertime means mango season,
Every Jamaican child goes wild, lose their reason,
In anticipation of the coming summer vacation,
When they can raid mango trees like St Julian,
Haden, Bombay, Blackie, Number 11, Stringy,
East Indian, Tommy Atkins, and Honey.
And if Mango galore wasn't enough reason
To play out of doors, we were definitely ditching our chores.

There were other summer fruits ripe for the pickings,
Naseberry, June plum, Guinep, and Otaheite apple, Coolie
plum, and Star apple,
Sugar cane, so sweet and divine, luscious custard apple and
sugar pine.
Who was lucky, head off to the country and reap watermelon off
the vine,

Raid farmer's fields of ripe produce ready for the picking,
Eat up grandmas' and aunty's finger-licking, country cooking.
If you were a 'Townie' living in Mobay or Kingston,
What was the typical city child's summer vacation?
Beach moves, drive out, backyard cookout and shopping trips,
Days out at Coconut Amusement Park or a family picnic on
Hope Garden grass.

You had to join in group games, you could not pass,
Skipping rope, Ring game, Simon Says,123 Red Light and
Dandy Shandy,
You better run fast in Shuttle Relay,
If you 'bat out' in Stucky, you can no longer play.
You had to go be 'Boatie' and if you couldn't manage that,
Go play Cricket or climb a tree whether short or tall,
How about Chinese Skip, Hopscotch, or Football?

Our parents didn't see us until it was time for bed,
At dinner time they called us, we were already well-fed.
We were scarcely hungry and rarely went home,
Darkness was the only thing that could get us inside,
Parents were superstitious and strictly forbade us to play in the
moonshine.
Duppy[1] and rolling calf[2] walk at night so come on in,
Duppy story at bedtime amused and frightened so 'till,
It was hard to fall off to sleep, too scared to turn off the light,
We were sure we could hear Duppy roaming outside.

Summertime was fun-filled days in the sun,
Days went so fast we cried when our 'free paper bun.'

1. Duppy - Jamaican Patios word for a ghost.
2. Rolling Calf - Jamaican folklore supernatural cow-like beast that appears
to be propelled along by flaming bands of fire.

It was time for detox, to purge out all the worms outta we,
With *Benjamin Herbs* and Bush Tea,
For strength and vitality, we drank Aloe Vera bitters, Neme, and
Cerase.
September morning off to school we went, everything shiny and
new.
New bag, every book on the book list, new haircut, and hairstyle
in fancy braiding and twist,
New uniform, new pencil, sharpener, ruler, exercise book and
pen,
New ribbon, new attitude and all who went to foreign come
back wid new accent.
Aww, boy! Summertime was the shortest six weeks in the sun,
We were so sorry when it was over, it was fun caa'n done!

Poem 16

THEY SAW ME

"Good morning Miss,"
"Morning Miss,"
"Good morning Miss,"
Lost in thought beneath the tall breadfruit tree,
Then came their happy chorus, as lovely as can be,
I was partly hidden behind the shrubbery,
And yet, as they passed my gate,
They saw me.

Their morning greeting resounded in a sweet chorus,
Enveloping me like a warm embrace,
They saw me even though they hadn't seen my face.
My presence was acknowledged, they affirmed I existed,
Yes, they agreed that I was there and worth acknowledging.
I was touched, I was overcome by a gesture so innocent of
agenda or guile,
Their warm greetings made me smile.
Oh! The manners of the typical Jamaican child.

My humanity was affected,
My existence confirmed by these simple but timely words,
I was flummoxed but managed to offer a belated reply,
"Good morning children, have a nice day,"
I waved as they happily walked by.

Looking over the fence, I studied their smiling faces,
Lovely, animated children walked with quickened paces,
Heading to school, immaculately turned out with care, bobbing
red ribbons in the girl's hair,
Pristine khaki and indigo uniforms ironed without a crease,
Epaulets, knife-like seams, and box pleats,
In retrospect, tears ran down my cheeks,
Remembering my own school days when
My teachers saw me.

How long had I been invisible on distant shores?
How many train commutes, how many revolving corporate
doors?
Harrowing *Tube*[1] trips, lonely walks in parks, exploring the
metropolis.
All alone never to be spoken to or acknowledged by anyone,
A contemporary ghost, ignored like an unwelcome apparition.
Indifferent clerks and guards, who would rather not speak to me,
Pointed annoyed, to signs, posted all-around, for all to see.
In that moment of standing by the gate underneath the
breadfruit tree,
The Jamaican children,
They saw me.

I savoured this greeting, tucked the meaning deep into my
heart,
I will have to pull it out whenever I'm back in England and feel
invisible again,
Their, "Good morning Miss," erased all my past hurt and shame,
This edifying message was imprinted in my mind,
I snatched it from the air vowing never to leave its dear memory

---

1   The underground train system used in England.

47

behind.
Unknown to them they sang a chorus, so robust, a truth so bold,
They said welcome home miss, welcome home from abroad.
Welcome home to Island life and sunshine kisses,
Here, greetings are as common as well wishes.
Bless them... They saw me!

Poem 17

100% CERTIFIED FOODIE!

100% Certified Foodie!
It stamp pon me forehead,
Look good and you will see;
100% Certified Foodie!
"If I don't love it, I don't eat it,"
Just like that food critique in *Disney;*
Don't carry any foolishness and come put down in front of me.
"Food is the staff of life," said Momma Cassie,
That's right, that means food must be fresh, healthy, and tasty.
A whe dis, nouvelle cuisine?
Muuum, it's lovely but lawks, it likkle bit eh?

Nothing to me like my yaad food,
You can never have your fill of it.
I'm no chef, I don't have the discipline for it,
But I'm a great cook, I am always in the kitchen,
The only thing left for me to do is to sleep in.
He, he, he, have you ever been to one of my dinner parties?
You don't know what you are missing.
Good food knows no prejudice, no matter the culture or the
cuisine,
As long as it tastes good, I will cook it and eat it, seen?
Look here, don't get me wrong, me no wanga gut,
Me nuh liki- liki, me jus nuh naam, from any, an any, baddy.

Food memories are the best,
They get you through so much stress,
After a hard days' work, what can get you through,
Better than a tasty plate of food?
At the thought of something nice to eat,
You can't wait to leave work, get home and have it.
The trouble is, when I leave my **bam-bai**[1] in the fridge at home,
That is twice as nice when it is a day old,
And when I am ready to tuck in, someone's already eaten it for me,
Do you want World War 3?
You must be crazy if you think, you can touch my food
and still, be friends with me!
I don't mind sharing, I love to give you yours but please don't touch mine,
Every tub must siddung pon its own bottom and the same goes when we dine.

So many lovely things in the world to eat,
 I intend to sample them all,
Yes, that is my lifetime's quest and feat.
I have my food list: those yet to be tasted,
And those that I fondly remember and want to have again,
Good food 'round me can't ever be wasted.

I don't trust picky eaters, something must be wrong,
How do they expect to be fit and healthy if their appetite is not strong?
A skinny cook - that's definitely wrong,
I feel so strongly that I could break into song.
That means that they don't even eat their own food, kekekeke!

---

1. A portion of food left over specifically to be enjoyed later

So then, good people, why on earth, should we?
My interests are:-
Recipes, gadgets, ingredients, flavourings, condiments, and
accoutrements for the kitchen,
Everything and anything to make food finger licking.

Everyone who truly knows me knows without a doubt,
That most assuredly, I'm happiest when I'm doing 3 things:
-Cooking and singing
-Eating and entertaining
-Planning again to do the same thing.
As long as I have great food to eat, nothing will bother me,
I'm on cloud nine and live in blue sky world,
'Cuz, I'm 100% a certified foodie.

Poem 18

SUSHI SHY

Oriental in my orientation,
Parochial in my presentation,
I'm definitely not for everyone
But those who love, love me,
I'm like Sushi.

I won't grace every palette;
Some see raw fish and retch,
I'm perfect in a KETO diet plan,
And again that is not for everyone,
There's a niche that will always go for Sushi;
Just like me!

Raw and uncensored,
What you see is what you get,
Complete with condiments and garnishes,
Rice fillings and seaweed wrappings,
There are no hidden surprises,
Once you've had it, without further ado,
You know Sushi is raw and true.

Protein-packed and full of goodness,
No sweet treats offered,
Here's a savory offering,

Wasabi as a throw-in,
You will avoid me if you are unschooled,
You will enjoy me if you are couth,
Unpretentious, bursting with nature's bounty,
That's Sushi and that's just like me!

Poem 19

PRAYER ON THE LANDSCAPE

I had a dream this last morning,
In the midst of the landscape of my Life
There is a place called prayer,
At first, I didn't see it,
But it was always right there.

I was wallowing around in my troubles,
I was crawling around on my knees and hands in circles,
Into the sodden ground, sinking my naked feet and bare hands,
I could feel the cool earth, smell the fresh rain on the watered
land.

Everything seemed alright with nature,
Everything seemed to be in God's perfect plan,
So what was wrong with me?
Why, I wondered, am I crawling around on my hands and knees?

I looked up and wondered how come I didn't see it there?
In the middle of the landscape of my life was a small shed called
prayer,
Who had built it, who had put the sign on it?
I have no idea.

Very rustic, but still solid and standing proudly for all to see,
I hurried towards it,

In my heart, I knew that was the place for me.
A warm shelter from the cold,
A certain refuge in the midst of adversity,
Prayer was always there but if I hadn't looked up,
Its proximity would have been lost to me.

So, if you are overwhelmed by troubles,
Wandering around in despair,
Lift your head up, survey the landscape,
Very close to you is a refuge called prayer.

Poem 20

LORD HAVE MERCY

People use this expression rather glibly; usually, if they have heard bad news or experienced a shock. It became a prayer to me one day when I realised that the sound track of my life was littered with constant complaining and nitpicking at God. I was really convicted and thereafter this expression became a heartfelt prayer. Written the 8th of February 2021.

I complained about a blemish, a spot on my face,
Until... I saw a man who was in a far worse condition.
He was faultless in a road traffic collision,
His entire face, engulfed in flames.
How can I dare complain?
Lord, have mercy on me!

Previously, I'd complained about so many trivialities,
Nothing to wear, not enough room to spare,
Needing another car parked outside my door,
The need for another manicure.
All these things are petty, they are of no priority,
God remove this complaining spirit from within me!

I didn't like this or that, I'd never wear that colour,
Then I came to grips with vulnerable people without justice and
power,

Abandoned children on the street, homeless people with
nothing to eat,
How much indignity do the elderly in nursing homes have to
endure?
Lord, I have so much to be thankful for.

A roof that shelters me, I can don my PJs and slip beneath clean
sheets,
I am full to contentment with good food to eat,
I have several shoes to shod my feet.
I have a loving, caring family and good friends,
If I ever complain again,
Lord have mercy on me!

Some have great trials, others seemingly have not,
One thing to be sure is that you can't tell what someone has
endured,
Unless you have been in their shoes, along their pathway
sojourned.
Accept and be thankful for what you have got,
I'm learning to be content with my lot.
Thank you, Lord, for Your mercy on me.

God never gives you more than you can bear,
Remain thankful, remember to share.
Be thoughtful of others, treat strangers with loving care,
Angels may come 'a calling,'
If you mistreat them that would be appalling.
Lord have mercy!

Now I look in the mirror I see my face,
I see a reflection that tells me, I am growing in grace,

I am ever so grateful for all that You have done,
I cringe now when I recall how I was so complaining and
tiresome,
Deep inside, I was so embarrassed that I chose to change,
Lord, please keep changing me!
#LordHaveMercyonme

Poem 21

OMG-4 REAL?

"Oh my God!"
So you know Him? He's My God I love Him!
What, you're not a Christian, you have no religion?
Oh! I see, just an expression.
I'm so hurt, so disappointed,
He's really dear to me, ever near to me,
He's my King, my everything.
So you don't even believe in Him;
You aren't interested in following Him?
Why then do you call on Him?

Seems incongruous to call on God,
If you are not even religious.
What's all the fuss about?
Okay, let's talk it out.
He is God, yes, above all you can ever think or imagine.
He's not an apparition,
He transcends explanation.
The miracle is, I know Him, experience Him,
Talk to Him and above all, serve Him.

No, He doesn't need me to defend Him!
The question is do you really want to offend Him?
I wouldn't mess with someone I didn't know,

There is no sense in that.

Be wise, approach with caution, treat with respect like a diplomat,

Today you may be bragging and boasting,

Tomorrow life may leave you coasting.

In your hour of need, you may really have to call on Him.

Would be great to know that you have not blown your last chance of Him answering.

Poem 22

DUMB AND NUMB

I looked at a photograph posted online of a wooden sculpture of a post with a bent hammerhead that had driven a nail into its own shaft. I considered this photo for a few moments and realised that there were instances in my own life that I was equally 'dumb' and thereafter 'numb' from being self-impaled. Written the 8th of September 2021.

Self-inflicted injury,
A cycle of pain,
Soul-destroying agony,
It was I who drove the nail,
Unlike HIM who bore in agony
My debauchery and shame,
Foolishly, carelessly, I became
Unceremoniously, self-impaled!

Writhing in agony, Oh my soul do be still,
Hoarse from screaming, a cry so shrill.
Compounded stupidity, self-indulgent and self-willed,
Instantaneous gratification, overloaded sensory landfill,
Dumping shredded emotions and crash-landed dreams,
Devastated mind, discombobulated body, and desperate
screams.

Who, who is to blame?
Rifle through your pockets,
Flip through your files,
Scroll through phone contacts,
Pick a name!
Evidence points to my very own name,
"It was you!" My conscience shouts back,
It was I, who was to blame.
I was so dumb then, what was I thinking?
Clearly, I didn't think;
Having let go of reason, into despair I was sinking.
Numbness rendered me incapable of pulling out that wretched nail,
Will I be subject forever, to be self impaled?
Please, somebody, help me!

Poem 23

PS* IT WASN'T LOVE

◆

This was possibly the hardest chapter of my life to think about and I'm so grateful for this poem as a means to express the emotional confusion, the soul searching, the spiritual agony, and the absolute joy in my realisation that it was merely a part of my journey, not my destination. Having found love at last I cherish it supremely; no poor copy can come near the reality. To my teenage readers, and more mature 'sistahs' and brothers, forgive yourself for your relationship mistakes, they are not the end, life has so many more takes. Written the 9th of September 2021.

To all the boys I've 'loved' before,
Ps* It wasn't love,
Pubescent chemistry, hormonal intensity,
Teenage exploration and curiosity,
Questions about life and sexuality,
These were all it was to me.
PS* I didn't know love.

Your constant pursuant nagging, pressing me,
Your claims of admiration for my body,
All fell on deaf ears.
You exposed your puerile, needy, greedy, lust to me,
PS* I knew that wasn't love.

Let's get married, we'd make a great couple,
Don't you agree?
Let's have a batch of children, two, maybe three,
I know we'd be good together you and me.
Sorry, Luv we're friends, we'll never be family,
PS* I'm still not in love.

My guarded heart shattered the moment I gave it to you,
My one life regret, I knew it was too good to be true.
In my heart, I knew It couldn't have been you,
You claimed you were obsessed with me,
That's the scariest thing anyone has ever said to me.
PS* We were definitely not in love.

No regrets, chalk it up to life experiences,
You had your way, I made my choices,
At the end of the day, no matter what anyone says,
Our 'romance' was fake,
No matter how many outings together,
How many great dates,
PS* It wasn't love.

Poem 24

MAYDAY-MAYDAY, SOS!

In 2017, I had a workplace accident. I fell off a faulty chair and damaged my hip, lower back discs, and coccyx. To say I lived in constant pain was a euphemism. I was bedridden for a while and I had to decide If I was gonna just lay there or fight to get back normality in my life. It took 3 years in total to get back to 'normal' and I had to lose 20 kg to get there. Now the problem was keeping the weight off by remaining disciplined. It was going to take a lifestyle change. I had a good 18-month go and I hit 50 years old and my world fell apart, again. Peri-menopause turned my world upside down and around and I felt as if 'my ship' had literally run aground after a battering storm. Hormones had me on a see-saw of weight gain and loss. I didn't know what to do. Everything I tried just didn't work. I needed help as the weight gain meant a relapse to my place of constant pain... Written during COVID-lockdown on the 3rd of February 2021.

Mayday-Mayday SOS! This ship is in distress,
OH God help me, I'm down, man overboard!
Oh God, I'm about to drown, in my desperation,
This is an SOS -Oh Lord save my soul!
I'm so overwhelmed, I'm losing control.

Save me from my own indiscipline,
My soulish rebellion is lingering STILL,

The REAL enemy is the heart of me,
That won't remain fixed on You.
I'm so distracted, my protracted inconsistency,
My complacency, my serial procrastination,
Is literally about to be the death of me.
Help me, Father! I don't want to die prematurely.

I know deep, down inside that You are sovereign in my life,
You are determined to perfect me,
I've got to stay focussed on You, Your word, Your plan, and
purpose.
Each day I arise, I must crucify my flesh,
Yes, eat less!
Walk More!
Keep healthy food in store!
It's pointless crying," I'm fat, in pain and dying,"
IF I DON'T STOP:
Finding an excuse,
Compounding my self-abuse,
Complaining incessantly,
Allowing indiscipline to live in me.

FEAR go, get out! Do you hear me shout?
I'm not going down with the count,
I'm gonna be the last one standing.
Oh God, that's my plea... Help Me! Help Me!
To conquer this indiscipline inside of me!
Thank you, Father, Amen!

Poem 25

PEOPLE CHANGE

Dedicated to Milton McCulloch, my brother poet and dear friend who said to me years ago, "Angie just write, begin and keep going." I'm grateful he never stopped asking if I was done yet. When I told him I'd begun this project he said, "Here is a phrase to work on as well - People Change." While we were having our Facebook conversation I was busy penning these lines in the background because I heard them in his words. Written the 4th of September 2021.

People Change,
They never stay the same.
For better, for worse, people change,
Seasons change, one day never remains;
Your joy today could later be your sorrow,
Today was once your tomorrow.
But come what may one thing remains and that is, change.

Sunshine this minute and in a while a downpour of rain,
Years of mental clarity and then dementia came,
Don't panic, you are always evolving, God's always transforming,
One thing is certain you too will change,
Why shouldn't you, do you really want to remain the same?
Frustrated with your circumstances, depressed by limited finances?

Trust God to turn things around, when you begin to change.

After the hard-earned degree,
You are no better off in your chances,
No better results in sought after romances,
Of this one thing, I'm certain,
If you hang in there, one day will be your curtain.
People change because God isn't finished until we are
perfected,
Don't get down on yourself, don't feel rejected.
Change is coming, I know for sure,
Don't resist it, don't reject it, go with the flow.
Change has got a grip on you,
Don't be afraid, change is good for you.
Every day, people change!

Poem 26

YOU ARE MY THERAPY

This poem came flowing out of me when I sat across from its subject, my darling husband Homer. I sat there intently watching the handsome figure of him as he worked quietly in his own mental space; a reassuring presence, a living testimony that it's wise to marry your best friend, and true love really never ends. Written the 20th of September of 2021.

Your voice from across the room so easily discernible and
distinguished from all others,
Above the chatter and clamour,
My heart knows it's you.
I am reassured by your proximity, I am excited that you are
somewhere in my immediate vicinity,
My head is cluttered with indiscernible thoughts and muddled
emotions that I can't express with any clarity.
You, again and again, you are in my head, finishing my
sentences, and then,
You speak sense and sensibility.
Dismissing any thought of momentary insanity,
Your voice is my therapy.

Your touch is a cornucopia of nature's blessings, butterfly kisses
trailing down my spine to my feet,
Your sniffing and inhaling a lung full of me,
Your pressed kisses upon my forehead brings such radiant heat
to my cheeks,
Massaging away all the tension from me,
Your hands in the small of my back leading me,
Supporting me while out in company.
The way your fingers trail down my nose, fondle my earlobe,
explore the skin of me, grooming me,
Your deliberate, accidental brush past me,
You just had to walk next to me, sit with me.
You warm my hands when I'm cold,
Nudge me forward to be bold.
Your touch is my therapy.

Raging turmoil within me, anxiety, emergency,
Your voice over the phone -instructive -decisive, focussing and

calming me,

You are on the pulse of my fear, at the command centre of every catastrophe,

You are my Gibraltar;

You take the lashings of the waves instead of me,

You pinpoint the epicentre of my tectonic tsunami,

You bear the consequences for me, covering for me so that I'm not treated like driftwood.

When I've been devastated and misunderstood,

You collect me, defend me, preserve my dignity,

You love me, you cherish me,

You are my Therapy.

AUTUMN

Nature does not hurry, yet
everything is accomplished.

Lao Tzu

What Autumn Means To Me...

Autumn is like a new Spring when nature does a wardrobe change. Autumn is a diva; she changes wardrobe just because she can. I love this about Autumn when the leaves change and they take on a whole new palette of colour.

It is my favourite season; I am in the Autumn of my life and loving it. I am old enough to know better and choose to be better. I am grown, I don't have the tolerance for the superfluity of naughtiness and foolishness. However, I don't dare to be proud; I am more considerate of other people's struggles and pain because I have the memory of my own. I don't have to explain or excuse myself. I've learned my lessons well and I'm open to learning new things every day.

So at this stage of my life, I'm a queenager. It's my prerogative to change my mind. It is like my last hurrah! Like an encore before its curtains. Autumn to me means stocktaking and leaving a legacy.

Poem 27

AUTUMN DAZE

The last flower of Spring has sprung,
On the eve of Summer the skylark song is sung.
While the sun sets over the horizon an orb of orange purple
haze,
I'm lost in an Autumn daze.

My youth is far spent, my passion and zeal is wavering;
I reminisce on the brilliant colour palette of long hot Summers
past and the former bounty of Spring.
Relishing auburn laden, copper sunset trees, the earthen
wholesomeness of yellowing fallen leaves,
Finding contentment in the limey green, pistachios, and burnt
orange accents that autumn brings.

Running through an arbor of golden trees and rolling on an
organic carpet of fallen leaves,
Arms like propellers flailing,
Trunk-like bodies tumbling down a hillside of memories.
Settling into a valley of reality.
Coming to terms with the fruitlessness of Summer romances
long extended,
Embracing Autumn's willingness to pacify the pain of unrequited
love, cruelly suspended.

The chill of Winter breezes, tease my cheek, taunting Autumn away,
The threat of snowfall transforms majestic branches laden with leaves into twigs,
The smells of blossoms are carried away on the winds,
Tall conifers stand at attention dressed in evergreen,
The grey clouds of Winter come rolling unceremoniously in,
Drenching the beauty pageant of nature, that Autumn is.

Poem 28

SCREAMING INTO THE WIND

❖

A summary of the events of September 2009 to June 2012.
This period was an initiation into the Autumn of my life. I finally
stopped being afraid to live life fully, to face changes and leave
the past behind. I was no longer too afraid to try things on my
own, to live my life the way I know God wanted me to. I'd given
myself so fully to everything I'd done in the past but it was a life
on others' terms and in service of others' visions and dreams. I
have no regrets or lingering acrimony; I facilitated and saw some
awesome realisations and transformations happen for others.
Now, it was my turn to fully and freely do me. I had to start again
but this time stand alone and believe in what God was doing in
me. Written the 24th of June 2012.

On the edge of this blissful shore I stand resolute and self-
willed;
The sands beneath my feet are receding and all nature is very
still;
Everything that is within me is screaming into the wind.

I see the billows rolling, folding, piling, and climbing ever still,
Turquoise towers terrify me,
They advance skimming the sky;
My ant-like form is confounded,
Transfixed, convinced I am going to die.

Then in that moment of stark reality, my mortality finds peace,
In the sweet surrender that nullifies retreat;
So I dig my toes more firmly into the sand beneath my feet,
And screamed as loudly as one could ever scream,
"TO LIVE IS CHRIST AND TO DIE IS GAIN!"

Fear flees as praise and worship comes flooding in;
Carried away by the backwash of the tempest;
To the sweet Rock of Ages I cling;
My anchor holds secure;
My soul unites with its Creator
On the mountain top of revelation;
The battering storm is no more.
The Spirit is but a whisper;
The welcome embrace of a faithful friend;
A new life in me is beginning where I once thought it would
end.

Poem 29

REALITY DAWNS

Reality is the other side of deception; like the heads and tails of a coin. One is more stark and the other less bold but one thing I know is that we need to embrace this duality in life. We cannot navigate life based on a lie no matter how sweet and soothing the deception, it will never deliver us safely to our destination. We are doomed to be tossed, shipwrecked and battered if we do not fix our eyes on the compass of truth and face the stark reality of life. Written the 23rd of August 2012.

Reality creeps upon us like a new day dawns,
Stretching itself across the skies of our horizons and as it yawns,
It exhales, breathing streaks of colour that illuminates the dull grey night,
Sweeping away the shadows that have haunted our thinking,
Evaporating the fog that had dampened our hopes and dreams.

Reality is a welcome, warm embrace to the seeker of light and truth,
A liberation from deception's dark jail.
Its rays of light are like the loosening of chains that once held us captive,
In dungeons of self-doubt and disbelief.
It is yet the foe of the unwilling, the lover of banal vanity,
Whose only true purpose is to enslave the soul;
But its captive knows no other master,

And, to its oppressive bidding remains cajoled.

Reality, you are faithful for with clockwork certainty you come,
Surely you follow each night with your luminous day,
Breaking the silence of fear, releasing the cries of untold grief,
Whitewashing dark clouds of midnight melancholy away,
Awakening the bird song that gives liberty to the wounded
soul,
Giving courage to the traveller to again take to the long dusty
road.

And yet, unwelcome or not, wherein there is still sorrow
From the burdens and trials of old,
Each time your fresh warm light shines upon us,
We embrace your truth, for it is undoubtedly,
Nourishment to the poorly soul.

Poem 30

THE MASQUERADE

*This poem was written in the Autumn of 2013 and had nothing
at all to do with COVID-19 and yet, it couldn't be more
appropriate now in 2020, during the COVID-19 pandemic, where
people are obliged to wear masks. I was concerned, at the point
of writing this poem, with the lack of honesty, forthrightness and
integrity around me. I've seen the following statement, posted
on social media which I paraphrase. "We [now] have to wear
a mask by law but many people [already] wear two by choice."
Author unknown. Uncanny right?*

Look! People are staring, they're upset with you,
You have no mask, you're out of costume.
Snubbed for having broken with convention,
Their remarks drip with condescension;
Your offense is noted for future recrimination.

Where then can I find acceptance if not in the company of my
peers?
In the fellowship of family and fellow believers?
In the warm company of loved ones of bygone years?
Who then will stop this charade, end this parading of parody?
I'll dare to don honesty and bare face as my garment;
Instruct the conductor to play a tune of delightful release,
And throw off all inhibitions to find pulsating peace.

Hear now the raucous sounds of souls set free;
Jubilant in their newfound liberty.
All masks have been abated,
Conductor, orchestra and guests satiated;
And the instigator has become the hero;
As our dance brought the King great pleasure.

As the music fades, they all fall away,
Each to their corner of reflection;
What an event! What an experience!
Why didn't we always do it this way?
Why did we ever choose the masquerade?

The certainty of honesty;
The discerning light of integrity;
Dispelled all opportunity for dalliances with impropriety;
A safe haven of importunity;
Where the knowledge of the character,
Of each soul present brought peace,
And judgement was silenced as truth left no room for critique.

I wonder, if I had camouflaged my identity,
And not dared to come to the ball, as me,
Would the King have chosen to dance among us,
Would we from the masquerade ever be free?

Poem 31

KEEP IT REAL

Keep It real,
Life is circumstantial, data must be tested,
Don't live life by what you see and feel;
Trust the truth that you know and have tested,
Depend on it like a frame of steel,
Keep it real.

See here now, this one is coming with all their fakery,
Wrapped around them like fine drapery,
Say what, you impressed by that?
You *Gucci, Dolce & Gabbana*, you *Prada, Burberry*, or you *Bradley*?
Name brand or not, it will rot, it can't last, won't get past eternity.
Reality is more than that, it is hidden deep inside each man.
Keep it real.

You there, in your dashiki, strutting like Professor *Rafiki*,
You ever been to Africa, you know anything 'bout them down there?
I'm asking you sah, have you ever been to the continent, Breda?
Woohoo, I know, I know you are reaching back to what is Black,
Yes, of course, Black is beauty but who are you?
Youth man, take it easy man, just take time and go through;
No matter the peer pressure, you have got to be you.
At the end of the day, you simply have to,
Keep it real.

How long have you been reinvented, been your best you?
Every day you are affirming and confirming, what/who?
You're still lost man, you don't have a custom-made plan.
Following the *Tweeters, Facebookers,* and the fakers on *Instagram.*
After decades of association here we are, I still don't know who you are,
Take it from me, while you aspire to be all you can be,
Just keep it real.

Your story changes every twenty four hours; this joke is gone too far,
Peering through filters, photoshopping, and cosmetic fixers to find you.
In an emergency will you be there for me, will you know me?
You walk past me on the street, head down in your gadget,
You daren't our eyes actually meet.
Your device is your life, you are an effigy, a walking hypocrisy,
I don't know you, you diplo-crite,
We best keep it real.

If you were my friend, you'd care about me, want to see me in reality,
Keep your thumbs up, I'd rather an, "Angel waz up?"
Oh, so I'm a dinosaur? I'm old school and live by the golden rule,
Yes, I treat others as I want them to treat me,
I need people in my life, I can touch and hug and love and see.
People who will let their hair down and relax and say, "This is me."
But I can't trust you in reality,
Maybe it's pointless asking you,
To keep it real.

$\mathcal{P}$oem 32

I AM SORRY

Facing our own iniquity is very hard; it's easier to hide behind professional, ecclesiastical and social facades. We play the game of charades really well, we delude ourselves with increasing proficiency and our lives become a lie. We can't grow until we choose to stretch upwards into the light of God's truth and photosynthesise into a planting of the Lord. We have to say, I am wrong, I am sorry, please forgive me and make things right. The moment I saw my true heart and faced my own weaknesses I knew then that if I'm wrong, I can't be strong. I cried out to God. He released my heart from guilt and frustration and I penned these words. Written the 25th of October 2021.

I am sorry,
It really isn't hard to say,
Not to you,
Today or any other day.
What is hard is facing the fact,
That I was the one who hurt you.
Yes, it's hard to accept that,
I had really done that.
Ah, yes, here comes that awful, sinking, feeling;
My head is reeling,
From the realisation that this mess we are in,
Originated with me,
From my iniquity.

I am sorry,
I mean it, I feel it, its breaking my heart
That is the easy part, to say it,
But what is really hard,
Is trying to delete the pain and the scars.
I'm not dodging my innate susceptibility,
I'm facing the foibles that still dwell within me,
I am so sorry.

Will these words set my heart free,
From the pain and misery?
Will it resolve the discord that now hangs between you and me?
I'm here to accept accountability,
To take responsibility,
For having allowed someone to come between you and me.
I want to make restitution to do what it takes to broker reconciliation.
Only then will the three words,
I am sorry,
Mean something to you and to me.

Poem 33

QUEENAGER

A bit of fun and laughter at my own antics, dedicated to all my sistah queens who are my peers and also to the youngins coming behind. I sincerely hope that you all learn not to take life too seriously but to enjoy life and live intentionally! Written the 4th of June 2021.

I went to the Queen's school,
I'm a King's daughter.
Called to reign and rule,
I don't need swagger or too much blabber,
Got my Father's substance and style,
I operate in decency and order.
Zero tolerance for nonsense,
Little sistahs, I've gotta tell ya
I'm a queenager!

I'm Grown but not old,
Don't let life age ya
Strut your stuff and belly laugh out loud,
Don't mock others, God resists the proud,
Stay humble! Yes, queens, you do you, I do me,
If we keep it on the level, we keep it real.
Keep it coming with cognitive stimulation, warm and loving vibrations,
Be honest and compelling, sensitive in truth-telling.

No competition here, conviction, motivation, earnest cheerlead-
ing,
For sure we got each other,
Little sistahs, I'm telling ya,
I'm a queenager!

As a queenager, I know lifes' roads, the bumps, and the curves,
The long straights ahead and I know when to swerve,
Been there, done that; I've got the T-shirt.
I don't need to throw shade or dish dirt,
I know well enough sistah, how much pain hurts,
So, I'd rather laugh out loud or giggle like a child,
Throw my head back and dance the electric glide,
Coming through with my grown woman wiggle,
Pulled up my *Bridget Jones*, snapped on that girdle,
Packed my comfy pumps and spandex to hold in my jiggle.
No matter what, Momma said, "Put your best foot forward,"
Nobody's fool, strong, bold, stepping out; no coward.
Life ain't over yet, I am still living with intent.
Why? Tell me why, oh why, would I grow up?
Even though I am grown, I am a contradiction the record has
shown,
It's my prerogative to change my mind,
I'm neither this nor that but a bit of both, and some,
How else can I tell ya?
Little sistah, I already warned ya,
I am a queenager!

Make room, move over, no messing around,
Move with alacrity, you will lose my attention, I get bored so
quickly,
Say it clearly, speak slowly, blah -blah- blah- Oh, I will soon for-

get,
Play my favourite song, I will know every line and dance to every set.
How else can I say it or persuade ya,
Of my age and make you believe?
Growing old is not an option, aging we can't do much about,
Old folks you can with all due respect, jog on!
This is for the young at heart,
Those not afraid to topple the apple cart,
Those not worried about breaking some outdated taboos,
Silver surfers get on your surfboards,
Party starters come in your hoards,
Life's too short and Winter is coming.
Make the most of hot, exciting Summer,
Enjoy life while Autumn leaves are yet falling,
There are many more adventures yet, I'll wager.
Get ready, set, let's go, all queenagers!

Poem 34

LAUGH AGAIN!

❖

My very best sistah-friend, Sharon Samms- Bett, was grief-stricken from the loss of her siblings and I felt so helpless to ease her pain. What could I do or say? I pondered, prayed and waited and then this poem came. Written the 25th of June 2013.

I don't have kin to grieve for,
I guess you of all know that's true,
But you are my family the one I'd give my blood for,
I smile at life because of you.

Sibling memories I guess would have been nice,
Learning to share and care, getting into trouble being told off,
But since we had none of these together I don't even think twice,
They would only be irrelevant if I had not spent them with you.

Heartbreak, I've surely had some and you have had yours too,
But what gets me through life's stress and trauma,
Is to know that come what may,
I will always have you.

So when you reminisce over your journey and all that you've been through,
Don't you ever feel guilty that you survived,
When your brother and sister didn't pull through.
I know you miss Marlon and Shani,
They lived their lives, had their own destiny, and so do you.

I know your road is often dusty, sometimes feels empty,
But it is taking you via the straight and narrow to the blessings that you are due,
I don't even have answers and I often act like a fool,
But I'd gladly be your jester if it will make you laugh,
Yes, when you laugh, I love listening to you.

Seasons come and bring their sorrow and pain, they also bring their rain,
Remember this one thing, in the rainy season without the pelting, splashing, raindrops there would be no bounty in the Spring.
You have always been my sunshine, a welcome snowdrop on a sun-baked plain,
And I'd face any storm or tempest,
Just to hear you laugh again.

Poem 35

SELFIE MANIA

My husband and I have been in ministry for over 30 years and yet we have grown closer to God, in the past 7 years compared to all that time. The Holy Spirit made us realise that we had more wicked ways in us than we would have liked to think. You see it was not our assessment of our lives that mattered, it was GOD's. He showed us how 2 Chronicles 7:14 reveals how we had picked up attitudes, traditions, doctrines, prejudices, biases, belief systems, cultural and popular practices that offended HIM, so we let them go. We let self die.

We go about our business tasks, ever mindful of our things to do,
We've become so self-obsessed, we live in a constant photo-shoot.

We are so busy taking selfies that we have taken ourselves out of the moment,
We may have captured the images but the spirit of it is lost, now a mere token.

When did it begin, where will it end?
This constant, peer pressure to take selfies un-end?
Do we have to follow every single trend?

It is lovely to take photos, they are great momentos,

but I scroll through my camera and all I see are hundreds of selfies of ME.

Yes, we are still a work in progress but we must have our priori-
ties right,
We have become our own IDOL that can't be pleasing in God's
sight.

I am grateful for the Holy Spirit's conviction, guidance, and
Grace,
To overcome my iniquity and my obsession with my own face.

Live intentionally as Jesus did and taught the disciples to do,
Go where we are sent, do what we are told we are supposed to.

Do not run off with another of man's 'BIG ideas,'
Align with Kingdom purpose and God's ways.

Everything else should be erased,
Especially our obsession with our own face.

Poem 36

DIAGNOSIS: VERBAL DIARRHOEA

Huuum... clearly your insides are churning from a diabolical infestation,
Your heart is definitely poisoned from toxic deposits,
I see, you are choking on your tongue, now heavy from the tales you have spun.
Do you have spasms and cramps that threaten to soil your pants?
Which end are you typically spewing from?

Oh dear, your mouth is bubbling over the edge of the wicked cauldron
That is your palpitating, calculating, heart,
That's been set boiling from the flames of hell.
Try to recall every unnecessary tidbit of juicy gossip.
How much did you chew on it?
Well, every piece of information that you chewed on,
Every person's dignity that you publicly trampled on,
Every rap sheet that you made;
Every confidential detail you liberally displayed,
Ruined lives and separated loyal friends.
Now the consequences are affecting you in the end.
Does your mind languish in an abyss of misery and malcontent?

From every symptom that you have disclosed,
From my experience I can confidently diagnose,

That you have, VERBAL DIARRHOEA!

Prescription: *See no evil, hear no evil and speak no evil.*
Do this everyday,
If you struggle, STOP and Pray!
Add reading the word of God as an immunity builder,
I can confidently guarantee you,
This is an antidote to your verbal diarrhoea.

Poem 37

TEMPLE KEEPING

Temple keeping, what is it?
It's all about being fit for purpose.
To be fit for purpose,
We have to be purposely fit.
That is, our bodies are God's temple and we must take care of it.

We have to take care of ourselves and live intentionally,
With the view of not allowing ourselves to die prematurely,
For the same reason, we cannot live casually and carelessly;
Not taking care of our spiritual, physical, and emotional health.
Where our body, soul, and spirit are left in need of maintenance
and spiritual wealth.

There is very little point in praying and fasting for the healing,
Of health problems when, we are eating and indulging,
In a lifestyle that is disease-inducing.
This is an imbalanced scale, God will simply not respond to
those prayers.
Those spawns of our serial disobedience, presumption, and
indiscipline.
There is no point in Bible reading if we don't apply the princi-
ples we are learning,
In our interpersonal relationships, applying them in our homes
as a beginning.

We must be conduits of love and understanding and willing peacemakers.
With this double standard, if we live like this, God will not hear our prayers.
We cannot plead ignorance before God -ignorance is not bliss.
Our lives will not yield fruit nor be purpose-filled,
We need to join God's boot camp and in the spiritual Gym get drilled,
Our inner temple light must get lit, with the Holy Spirit,
Feed on the living word, become like incense,
Become living praise, abiding in His presence.

Your body is His temple and God is the Lord of all,
He is a jealous husband,
He will not share His bride with any one at all,
So all idols must go,
Of the devil, God will make an open show,
He needs room to dwell, to show His power.
Temple keeping requires all of you, it's a lifestyle,
A lifetime's vocation,
A commitment that demands your full cooperation.

Poem 38

ORDER! ORDER! ORDER!

Bring the family into Your Order, Oh God!
Place the rule of Your Spirit deep within,
Bring the Community into Your Order, Oh God!
Purge the rebellion born of sin,

Bring the nations into Your Order, Oh God!
Mystery Babylon has intoxicated them to their chagrin.
Order begins in Your house, Oh God,
Order! Order! Order, within!

Order our minds and thoughts,
Change our carnal thinking,
Order our steps in Your Word,
Respectfully carrying Your authority,
Not just go rushing in.

Order! Order! Order!
Our words, our deeds, even the songs that we sing,
Let them lead us to, Your Mercy Seat,
To worship as the Cherubim.

Divine Order upon God's people fall,
From God's mountain top snowball,
Living Word, point the way to go,
Spirit wellsprings dug deep, overflow.

Order in alignment,
Rank and file,
Roles and functions in sync,
None left behind, left out, neglected, rejected,
ALL People of God, fall in!

Line upon Line,
Principle upon principle,
Your *Rhua* breathe,
Your *Rhema* bring,
Assign anointings, functions, and giftings.

A blueprint,
A master plan,
A tapestry,
A Picture,
A Divine Vision.

Your Glorious Bride,
Hidden in Christ we abide,
Your way of being,
Man's pride denied.

Poem 39

LOVE COVERS

This poem was written on the night shift some time in 2012, while contemplating how I should respond to the hardships my coworkers had created for me. Working with Young People on the Autistic Spectrum, among other learning difficulties, and physical disabilities was challenging enough as it was. The last thing I needed was to have to work with less than professional colleagues who made for an awkward working environment. I was frustrated all the time. I really wanted to quit but God said to me, "LOVE them." I realised that I had come to dislike them deep in my heart. I had to repent and ask God to give me a genuine love for them, not mere professional tolerance. I prayed and God gave me the grace. Things improved beyond my expectations. I was nominated by them for employee of the month. I didn't see that coming.

You confuse my gentleness with weakness,
You call me foolish because I am kind,
You don't appreciate my candour;
You get upset when I speak my mind.

You don't celebrate my integrity,
To other's deceit you are blind;
When I am quiet and introspective you would rather I take sides;
Yet you alienate me from your clique by setting the bar too high
and lower it for your own kind.

100

It's hard enough to please you as you don't know your own mind,
No matter how hard I work for you from morning until night,
My progress makes no difference, my due promotion is denied.
At every point of my journey, you are there to break my stride.

My indomitable spirit is not broken;
Joy soothes and strengthens my traumatised mind.
Hope in me is a spring eternal, willing me on to survive,
If I hated you that would be weakness and surely unkind,
It would cripple and destroy me, a mere placebo for my wounded pride.

Loving you has to be my answer, my modus operandi,
For only love offers redemption and the promise of eternal paradise.
So mock me in this lifetime,
Berate me and deride,
Love has been my portion, my solid anchor, and my guide.

A faithful companion no matter how dark the night;
Like the sun each morning love rises hot, full, rich, pure as light,
And it covers all the sins of mankind.

Poem 40

RACE?

This poem came from my notes compiled in preparation for an online discussion about Racism and its effects on the African diaspora. As I flipped back through my notes, the truth of each line began to speak to me and I wrote this poem. I hope it brings you clarity in these troubled times. Written the 7th of August 2020.

RACE...
Race is a misnomer; no such concept exists in God's mind;
As seen by His diversity in design.

One race on earth, one human being - the descendants of Adam.
The mind of God has one plan - unity in diversity,
Sensitive design - melanin as protection for the Equatorial Africans,
Less for those who don't need it, in the cooler temperatures, the Europeans.

Where did this notion of Race come from?
This slow poison we have been 'drop fed,' The one-drop rule?
This subliminal illusion and lie came from the demonic realm.
Lucifer's plan was thwarted at the flood when they mixed in demons with human blood. The human genome must never be compromised; So God washed the earth and began a reprise.

Here comes Satan again: slavery, oppression, greed,
Empire building, colonial domination.
'War open or understood' - John Milton's epic poem warned us,
Satan swapped the good,
Don't keep eating the fruit of deception and planting its seeds,
Wherever you hail from, this global village is the home of homo-
sapien,
One man, one woman, the seed of Adam.

One people IN Christ through the blood YESHUA,
In whom we in the Kingdom of God ABIDE,
Our existence is sacred, every life is precious,
The expression of God's pride.
Whatever we do, build unity, retain the truth,
As for RACE?
Mash down that lie!

Poem 91

TRACES OF YOU

Written for Cathay-Ann Clemetson, my covenant sister. It was going to be her birthday soon and it made me grieve our separation by migration, yet again. However, this time I had grown, I was no longer afraid to be alone and was bolstered by the legacy we share. I am not shattered by her departure anymore because I know she will always be near me in my heart. Written the 10th of October 2020.

Traces of you,
Are in everything you touch,
In everything you do,
There is a trace of you.
Everywhere you go you leave traces of you.

The unmistakable essence of your style,
Your way, your grace,
The beaming smile upon your face,
The kindness in your eyes,
The eloquence of your meaningful silence,
Your presence leaves a signature of indelible excellence.

All around my life you have left a trace,
In rooms, in gadgets, in trinkets,
In gifts of quality and fine taste,
Yet none as costly as the shared moments,
The memories together that time cannot erase.

The food you prepared, the prayers said,
The timely visits, all showed how much you care,
There's a special place in my heart that no one can fill,
So although you are there and I am here,
The traces of you linger with me still.

Poem 92

LIFE LESSONS

Life lessons is a summary of the principles that I have learned over these last 5 decades. Some of these lessons were pleasant and others quite painful. You know we have three ways of learning in life. One is by observing the mistakes of others and drawing the object lessons from their example. The second way is to conduct independent research around a matter and arrive at our own conclusions or choose to make our own mistakes. Lastly, we can choose to follow the instructions of an authoritative source that is considered quite credible. I've learned these principles in all of the above ways but I highly recommend that we learn, regardless of the methodology, as we are all different and life's circumstances are always changing. Be a quick study in the school of life and be prepared to learn, change, and live fully, not merely exist.

Faith in GOD IS PREEMINENT in life.
INVEST IN PEOPLE, not things.
HEALTHY RELATIONSHIPS are not subject to time/space nor are they altered by success or disgrace.
FAMILY is not just blood relatives BUT NURTURING RELATION-SHIPS,
REAL FRIENDS ARE LIFELONG through thick and thin.
BE PRESENT in the moment it goes by so quickly.
You DON'T REALLY NEED all the stuff you think.

NEVER say never, life is constantly changing;
Variables CHANGE and circumstances alter situations.
THINK about the big picture...You are not the only priority.
DON'T GET TOO ATTACHED to this planet it's gonna end soon.
The future is in God's hands and HE'S MORE CAPABLE than
you.

FOCUS AHEAD, being preoccupied with your past puts your
future in jeopardy,
EMBRACE PYJAMA DAYS, taking a break and resting is the best
therapy.
YOU CAN'T navigate life, based on a lie, so face the truth and
get on with it.
It is NOT YOUR JOB to fix people, leave them to their Creator
who knows them best,
Prayer changes things, talk doesn't always; sometimes it MAKES
THINGS A MESS.
Timely silence is golden, YOU CAN'T TAKE BACK words that
were badly timed and poorly expressed.
So just LISTEN MORE AND SAY LESS, you'll be guaranteed less
stress.
EVERY DAY IS A SCHOOL DAY don't waste 24 hours by not
learning at least one new thing.
DON'T DISCRIMINATE against your teacher, wise and powerful
people are often unassuming.
BE TEACHABLE, you can be taught by people, circumstances,
and nature.
Take in information like a sponge, you never know WHERE,
WHEN or HOW FAR it will take you.
LEARN YOUR LESSONS WELL, don't keep perpetuating the
same old mistake,
When all is said and done, more is usually said than done;
So, PRAY more than you SAY!

WINTER...

No winter lasts forever; no spring skips its turn.

by Hal Borland

What Winter Means To Me...

Winter is coming... I can feel its encroaching chill in the crisp wind. Winter means to me what is ahead. I really have no idea what the future holds. Jamaicans have a saying, "Only God can see around corners." Winter is around the corner for me. Winter means preparedness and expectation and the faith to trust that it is going to be God's best.

Winter means the warmth of trusted companionship, reward, and rest.

Poem 93

PURPLE

Purple majesty, pomp, and pageantry,
The colour of royalty.

Purple passion splashed across the horizon,
Sunset splendour.

Purple flower, violet and vibrant,
Lavender and fragrant.

Purple punch, grape and sweet,
Spirited or neat, delicious distillery.

Purple pumps, satin and cute,
Soft leather boots.

Purple hues, everywhere,
Purple smells fill the air.

Purple, what would I do,
Without the calming comfort of you?
I Just love you Purple!

Poem 44

P IS FOR PINK

A tribute in Poetry to the late Janet Pink, a pretty flower from God's garden picked too soon. Written the 27th of February 2021.

Pink- a lovely colour that comes in all shades and varieties,
But is still so undeniably and predominantly
The colour that suits you my friend 'Pinky.'

P is for Precocious
Well ahead of her peers,
Showing maturity beyond her years,
Our very own 'Shorty' and 'Miss Feisty',
The BIG little woman with such passion and tenacity.

P is for Perseverance
You kept fighting and knocking on Heaven's door,
You pushed through, you endured, you never gave up,
No illness, no disability could make you stop.
Being the Janet everyone adored.

P is for Propriety
A 'proper' British lady, no 'slim shady,'
She wasn't the sort to 'spill the tea,'
She had your back,
She was a real friend to you and me.

P is for Priceless
The piercing peals of her laughter, echoing and filling the
space,
It was well as long as she was laughing with you and not at you,
Then I would really feel shame for you,
Yup, go hide your face...

P is for Perceptiveness
She could sniff a fake a mile away, she could always turn your
night into day,
Of what she saw and what she knew,
She'd be the first to tell you the truth.
Because you knew her pure intent, you felt safe in what she said.

P is for Precious
Precious aptly describes you to me,
When I remember Janet
Who was unlike any other,
So full of love and vitality.
You are gone from us,
But will never be forgotten by us.

P is for Promise
Our hopes are wrapped up in the promise of your eternity,
We imagine how much you are enjoying your immortality,
Thinking of your days of bliss and wonderful contentment,
Gives us such joy, until we will see you again.
'Likkle more' Pinky, 'walk good,'
Our sister and friend!

Poem 95

THE PAPER STAIRCASE

Delicate origami, delightful and pretty,
Innovative, intuitive, sample of human ingenuity.

Towering high, upon your treads my aspirations climb,
Will you sustain these weighty expectations of mine?

Is your beauty an enticement my footsteps to deceive?
Will you hold me in grief, bolster my reprieve?

Paper staircase, you are built on a fallacy;
Truth blows upon you exposing your heresy.

Your spiralling banisters a kite-like fantasy, blown away with
whim and fancy;
Your foundation is judged insecure, having no leverage to endure.

Justice is a sword that like a pendulum swings,
In judgment, it destroys you for the desolation you bring.

Consoled now by the truth of yore,
Trusting only in things that endure;
Just like truth never grows old,
 A paper staircase will never hold.

Poem 96

IT'S OKAY NOT TO BE OKAY

I'm not holding it together,
Everything's too much, such a bother,
Oh my goodness did I really just say that out loud?
Father forgive me you know I'm not proud,
My eyes are brimming,
I'm counting to a hundred, ten didn't do it,
No one is really looking or listening,
I need to get through this,
Haven't they noticed that I'm not quite right,
I'm not being the real me?
It's okay not to be okay...
I heard the woman say.
The phrase hung in the air and I snatched it,
That's definitely meant for me.

I'm not okay, I'm irascible and grumpy,
I feel suffocated, I need to exhale.
I just need to breathe,
I really need to grieve.
We all grieve differently,
Listen to your heart,
Note the changes in your body.
Cut back on your schedule, pace yourself,
Just take some time to grieve.

You may be triggered by a memory,
You may blank out, get lost in a daze,
You may be hyper- sensitive and sentimental,
No two persons grieve exactly the same.

You may feel unhinged, unsettled, nauseous, even get ill
If you've become that temperamental,
Sit alone by yourself and just be still.
If quietness isn't helping you cope,
Cook up a storm,
Have friends over,
Eat yourselves silly,
Laugh and play until you are giddy.

Whatever medicates your pain,
Whatever gets the emotions out,
If it doesn't quite work, try something else
And keep doing it all over again.
Whatever it takes,
Have your pyjama days,
It's not your fault, no one is to blame,
And its okay, not to be okay.

Poem 97

ALONE IN AN EMPTY ROOM

Dedicated to the memory of my dear sister in the Lord and best friend Jennifer Wood who left this earth too soon, during this pandemic. I struggled with finding closure to her untimely departure. I felt like all the colour had been whitewashed out of my life. She took the colour and laughter with her. Not being able to attend her funeral and be with her family killed me silently, my heart just broke and I daren't openly express my grief, it was just too much and I didn't know how to get the pain out. This poem is as close as I have come to accept that she is gone. I miss her so much. Written the 25th of October 2021.

Jennifer, Jennifer where are you my boo?
I tried so very hard to get to you.
My heart broke when I heard that you have already left the
room,
My mind keeps repeating the same track on loop,
Gone too soon, gone too soon.

Oh, I was too late for us to get together,
To get on with things left undone,
Dances to do and songs yet to be sung,
Gone too soon, gone too soon.

Another day I'm still expecting to come round to yours,
Hang out, eat our favourite food, do some chores.
I'm taking up the phone, about to call you,
I just can't seem to remember, to accept
That you won't answer.
I wasn't prepared, I just wasn't ready yet,
Time froze, my heart stopped when I was told you left.
So I'm all alone in this empty room,
Because you are gone too soon.

Should I delete your contact, what do I really do?
How on earth am I supposed to go on without you?
I'm left standing here in an empty room that's been
Stripped bare, left brilliant white;
Because when you left, you took all the colour out of my life.
You are gone too soon, just gone too soon.

You left me here standing alone in this room,
Of memories and mementos and the pictures of the silly things
we'd do,

I'm left with the record of our days, our progress, our accom-
plishments, our milestones, our silly throwback looks,
In your photo album filled with the great 'pics' you always took.
Yet, I'm so empty because nothing compares to being here with
you,
In our special place, this room of memories of me and you.

I didn't get to say goodbye, see you or say to you, 'I love you'.
I wanted to see you off, to hold your hand,
By the time I got there, your train left the station,
You had already departed this land.
When you get there ahead of me, in God's great, big room,
Will you save me a seat, the way you always do?

Poem 98

JAMAICAN CHRISTMAS TIME

Christmas, my most favourite time of the year,
Filled with Childhood memories held so dear.
Island breeze but no Santa Claus or reindeers,
But a house filled with laughter and good cheer.

Mommas and aunties cooking up food galore,
Extended family comes piling through the door.
Children vying to snatch goodies laid out on the kitchen table,
Egging each other on to see who will be able.

Sorrel, eggnog, rum punch, ginger beer, everything for your
drinking pleasure,
J. Wray and Nephew are added for good measure.
Help yourselves, dinner is served, no one is a guest here,
Eat up, or we will have leftovers to feast into the New Year.

Curry goat, honey-glazed ham with pineapple and Maraschino
cherries,
Green Gungo rice and peas, Aunty Cathay's special macaroni
and cheese,
Uncle Clive's lasagna, jerk chicken, Donna's escovitch fish,
Mum's broccoli salad, our favourite side dish.

Please pass along the cranberry sauce, it goes with the ham,
I haven't had any dessert yet, I'm filled to bursting,

Leave space for the candied sweet potato, man.
Grandma baked Christmas pudding;
I'm having that next, sure thing!

Wow, what a mess, what's that chaos? It's Christmas, don't worry,
It's the children, ripping wrapping paper off their gifts in a hurry,
I've got a walking dolly! What did you get?
I've got just what I wanted, a train set.
My Peter Pan boots are so fashion-forward,
I'm really happy with my skateboard.

Much later on, well into the early morning hours,
The house is filled with kiddie giggles and adult snores,
Careful where you place your feet, there's a sleepy child under-
neath.
Bodies are snuggled up everywhere in front of the fire's heat.

Kingston dwellers complain that Stony Hill is cold and rainy,
Snuggled under blankets if they can manage to get any.
Pinecone smells emanate from the huge Christmas tree,
Mingling with the aromatic smell of charming cedar beams.

Ahh... the memories of my simple childhood joys,
Time-stamped on my heart, more precious than gifts and toys,
A Jamaican Christmas is more about family and good friends,
Maintaining relationships, warmth, and hospitality without end.

The fact that Christ's birth was His perfect gift,
Cushions our festivity and gives us such a lift.
We know that without God's goodness being employed,
We'd have literally nothing to celebrate and to be enjoyed.
Have a blessed Christmas... Jamaican style!

Poem 99

THE TRANQUIL WINTER

Modern Chinese instrumental playing in the background,
Cushioning my thoughts with its tranquil sounds,
Snow softly falling like icing sugar through a Patissiere's sieve,
Rhythmic tapping on the keyboard,
All is well in the world,
Nature is so still...

Snowfall makes the heart tranquil,
Freezes worry, makes the clamour of the world so still,
Frozen droplets of water so precariously shared far and wide,
Over frozen lakes and avalanching mountainsides;
Furry animals and clambering humans struggle to cope,
On slippery surfaces, and hilly slopes.

One in its natural habitat taking it all in stride,
The other seeking happy pastimes,
Skiing, rolling, sledding, and tubing in tow,
Making angel wings in freshly fallen snow.
The crisp, cold wind against my cheeks,
North Easterlies, bowing the naked sprigs of trees.

Sounds of nothing but the frosty wind,
Fills me with a deep knowing,
Winter tranquilizes me.
Hot breath against the windowpane,

The heart rejoices in the absence of chilly, wet rain,
Overcast, grey days and the quick darkness it brings,
Welcoming the snow-covered sod and the chilly song the wind
sings.

How reflective, how bright even against the descending night,
Fires crackling, logwood sparks, embers glow,
Radiating warmth that counteracts the chill of snow.
Families huddled in wool, clad with fleece,
Wintertime brings the soul calm and peace.

Poem 50

CONSIDERING THE MEANING OF LIFE

This brings us to the end of my 50 - year journey and there were so many lessons learned. I considered what my life really meant in the bigger scheme of things. I wondered, had I lived responsibly, would I leave a legacy worth commemorating? Have I been a role model? I spent time asking God for the answers to these questions knowing that I still had the gift of today and hopefully more tomorrows to make a difference to my sphere of influence. I knew I couldn't change the world but I could change me, as a start. Written 10th January 2022.

Considering the meaning of life?
Everything in life remains meaningless,
Insignificant until its divine purpose is revealed and understood,
When its significance to our lives and the world is realised.
Once it is realised, then it begins to impact the world for good;
Heals the brokenness of humanity,
It repairs the torn tapestry of life.
Until then it remains like a chess piece that has not been moved into position,
Like a ship in a doldrum blown off course,
In the end game of life.

We must come to know and understand the divine reason,
For the existence of people and things in their season;
Don't just go arrogantly stomping through the earth.

We may trample on the precious, extinguish the necessary,
Break the buttresses, remove the landmarks relied upon by
many;
Empty the dams of life and ignorantly hasten our own demise.

Rather we must humbly apply an enquiring mind and ask God,
What is the meaning of this?
Let's not rush away from His presence,
But wait for the reply, don't hasten action in impatience.
Until we are clear that we are an instrument of His divine will;
Seek His face, wait for answers and be still.

Only then, can our lives have true purpose,
When we know with certainty the reason,
God allowed our mothers to birth us.
Our steps are ordered, then we move with alacrity,
No stumbling and grappling for life's meaning,
No antipathy and self-indulgent sophistry,
We embrace life's seasons knowing they come with reason.

Author's Profile

Angela B. Slack has taught and trained across secondary and further education for twenty years; in both Jamaica and the United Kingdom. She developed specialism in Humanities, Expressive Arts, Communications, Curriculum Development, Instructional Design, Special Educational Needs, Worked Based Learning, Life Skills and Literacy intervention.

Mrs. Slack has written instructional resources across a wide range of technical, vocational and academic disciplines for the HEART TRUST/NTA Jamaica.

She has developed curriculum for the Schools in North Lincolnshire UK on the Black Peoples of The Americas.

Gifted in Creative Arts, Mrs. Slack has trained and coached chorales and drama groups, and has written dance dramas and a musical at an amateur and semi-professional level in a voluntary capacity. These groups have won awards and have enjoyed public acclaim. *Droplets of Water Shafts of Sunlight,* is her first collection of 50 poems.

She has retired from formal education and together with her husband is a co-founder and the Chairperson of **United in Christ Charity,** Managing Editor of **Select Arrow Publishing,** Editor of the **SHARE Magazine,** Curriculum Administrator for **Open School of the Bible** and works in Christian ministry alongside Homer Slack to whom she is married for 32 years. They are the parents of two adult children Dorian and Briana Slack.

Printed in Great Britain
by Amazon

80126296R00088